REVOLUTION

**When strange becomes normal,
and logic gets turned on its head**

Juan Manuel Muñoz

Wisdom
Editions
Minneapolis

Wisdom Editions

SECOND EDITION DECEMBER 2022

Revolution: When strange becomes normal, and logic gets turned on its head. Copyright © 2021 by Juan Manuel Muñoz.
All rights reserved.

10 9 8 7 6 5 4 3 2

ISBN 978-1-960250-31-5

Cover and interior design: Gary Lindberg

"You say you want a revolution
Well, you know
We all want to change the world..."

Excerpt from the song "Revolution"
–The Beatles

Table of Contents

Also by Juan Manuel Muñoz

From Primates to Politicians
(Wisdom Editions)

REVOLUTION

**When strange becomes normal,
and logic gets turned on its head**

Wisdom
Editions
Minneapolis

Chapter 1:
Introduction

*"Somewhere, something incredible is waiting
to be known..."*

— Carl Sagan

This morning, I watched as the waves rolled onto the sand, delighting in the beauty of the landscape. A white sand beach, merging with clear water that reflects the sky, as we usually imagine the beaches of the Caribbean. In the midst of this beauty, I thought: the sea looks calm, but there are still waves. Could it be that if the breeze stopped blowing, the waves would cease completely? Well, no. The forces that move the sea are multiple and dynamic. Certainly, the waves will continue to carry things to and from the beach, will continue to shape the coast, will continue to produce changes, just as everything around us is constantly changing.

I remember the scene now, late at night, and continue to wonder: Can anyone really believe that anything remains static? What in this world is static? If you stand motionless, you are still on the earth. The earth, with its radius of approximately 6,371 kilometers and a complete rotation on its axis in twenty-four hours, is carrying you along at the amazing speed of 1,668 kilometers per hour! The speed of sound is 1,234.8 kilometers per hour (traveling through air with a temperature of 20 degrees Celsius), which means that you are actually moving at a supersonic speed even as you stand there doing nothing, convinced that you are standing still, proud of how much time you can spend in this position, imitating a statue.

Okay, imagine yourself on a planet that does not rotate. If it revolves around a star like our sun, you may be moving at 30 kilometers per second (108,000 kilometers per hour), just like on Earth. That is more than eighty-seven times the speed of sound!

The most interesting thing is that these numbers are pretty much negligible when we consider that our sun revolves around the center of the galaxy at a speed of approximately 700,000 kilometers per hour, and that our galaxy moves away from other galaxies at approximately 72 kilometers per second (259,200 kilometers per hour).

I can't help smiling as I ask myself: Does anyone really want everything to stand still? Or for change to cease? Can anything really be stopped, or remain calm? Not to mention the speed of electrons in every atom of matter in every molecule of our body.

It seems that we are so busy checking the latest notifications on our cellphones, or worrying about getting home as we sit stuck in traffic, or just trying to get through our daily routine as best we can, that we don't seem to realize that each of us is nothing more than a single specimen in a colony of seven billion similar individuals of the same species. All inhabiting a wet rock that travels at incredible speeds through space. This means that if you consider yourself so special as to be one in a million, there are still 7,000 of your equals found the world over, thinking they are just as special as you. That is enough to fill entire schools, and certainly to fill hundreds of buses.

The exercise of thinking is a huge burden. Very heavy and very cumbersome to lug around. For no matter how long we spend trying to understand our place in this universe, we will never fully be able to do so. Not because of forces from beyond that prevent us, or because of the magical veil of mystery that protects the unknown from the contamination of the perverse human mind, but because of our limited mental capacity, which faces an unmanageable amount of information that is growing exponentially. Despite our ability to think abstractly we are not able to handle so much information simultaneously. The memory capacity of the human brain has been calculated at 2.5 petabytes (one petabyte is one million gigabytes), despite barely using the energy needed to light a dim light bulb.[1] As wonderful and unmatched as our brain machine is, we are condemned to know only a little about many things, or to know almost everything about almost nothing.

1   Ghose, Tia. "The Human Brain's Memory Could Store the Entire Internet." LiveScience. Purch, February 18, 2016. https://www.livescience.com/53751-brain-could-store-internet.html.

We simply cannot know everything, nor process all the information at once. Our limited intelligence feeds on limited senses, and is helped along by limited technology. Thus, where before a philosopher could master much of the useful knowledge generated up to his time, today, knowledge is so scattered and focused on specialties that the poor philosopher is reduced to barely grasping a portion of what is being said.

It seems that in dealing with even the most basic philosophical and ethical dilemmas, we have been overwhelmed to the point of not recognizing things that should be easy to identify, such as success. A few days ago, I was telling my medical students that I no longer know what or who is a successful person. Something as simple as "finding happiness" has been contaminated by our society with all kinds of material, vain and superfluous aspirations that often end up destroying us, harming our fellow man, and even hurting our environment.

If so, then why ponder the speed of the earth as it hurtles through space, or doubt the numbers I have mentioned? It has always been easier for people to believe and accept without discussion, or to sidestep a topic that makes them consume energy in such a seemingly futile fashion. It may not seem to them that they are moving as fast as what this book says, or it may be that they "believe" that things are not so because someone else told them differently.

In the end, I find it ironic that we search for signs of extraterrestrial intelligence or get caught up in the intrigue of whether beings from outer space visit us, when there are still so many mysteries right here at home to be answered about how our own brain and thought processes work.

There are times when I think we have resigned ourselves to no longer finding intelligence on our own planet!

Fortunately, we live in a time when it is easy to find, analyze and share information. But this was not always so. The ease with which we search today for a formula, or a figure, or detailed scientific information, is the product of advances in communications and computer technology. Many characteristics of our culture, in the way we meet our needs, were not as we currently know them; at some point there was a great shift that transformed them into what we know today. Sometimes this happened through acts of violence or peaceful protests; other times, through ingenuity and scientific advances, or simply through education. In short, throughout history humanity has been exposed to all kinds of changes that have shaped our fragile environment. An environment which, when viewed through our sense of immobility, seems to reflect a robust and unchanging reality. Everything seems fixed and durable, if not eternal.

The waves of the sea are all different. No two are exactly the same as they arrive on the beach the way they did this morning as I watched, entranced. The marks that remain on the glistening white sand are never the same, as no two scars on the skin are exactly the same. Likewise, no two social moments are exactly the same, in the midst of the whole movement of the universe.

Human phenomena do not escape the wild, dynamic fury from which we descend and of which we are a part. I find it frustrating and hard to understand why the field of human behavior continues to be addressed through superficial and diffuse studies while remaining shrouded by the thick veil of the unknown. If we are not yet able to understand the most wonderful and closest mystery we have, which is the functioning of our brain, how much more difficult will it be to understand the workings of several interconnected – or, to use a more popular term, synchronized - brains.

My first encounter with science was a book by Levi Marrero, *La Tierra y Sus Recursos* (The Earth and Its Resources). This was a geography book that included astronomy and concepts for understanding the universe, which I took from my mother's bookshelf at six years of age. My interest in science was further fueled by my father, who bought a telescope so that the whole family could observe the passage of Halley's Comet in 1986.

Over the years, the books I read continued to infect me with the vision of reality of men like Galileo Galilei, Rene Descartes, Albert Einstein, Stephen Hawking and Carl Sagan, as well as many other students of nature, the universe, our origin, and the human species. Nevertheless, even bright minds are not always right, and many times what little we know leaves us with more questions than answers concerning the nature of this knowledge.

Studies involving human behavior, institutions and society are commonly known as "soft" sciences. I cannot understand how there is anything soft in any discipline that seeks knowledge, or in any kind of science for that matter. The real difference between soft sciences and hard sciences seems to me to be the scientific rigor and the courage that is instilled in the formation of the presumed scientist who studies them. Perhaps we just need to be equally rigorous, meticulous and dedicated in the study of our behavior as a species.

Freedom is one of the most valuable things that we humans possess, but it is very difficult to embrace freedom of thought from the darkness of ignorance. Only scientific knowledge allows us the freedom to question, to decipher mysteries and to arrive at the truth. Science provides the tools that allow us to analyze the facts without resorting to attributing each phenomenon to a mysterious force. Unsurprisingly, things of value are often coveted as a means of achieving individual goals. The value of freedom of thought is so great that there are those who would unfortunately deprive other human beings of it. The freedom to think is taken away from people who have never had the chance to experience it and will probably die that way.

My previous book, *From Primates to Politicians* (which could just as easily have been called "From Primates to Primates," since there really isn't much difference), was born out of a curiosity regarding the political nature of human beings. This time around, I am driven by the need to understand how such a high level of refinement has been achieved in the manipulation of the masses. How a handful of individuals can decide the future of a majority that believes itself to be free, but generally is not. How small accidents in manipulation have resulted in out-of-control situations, some leading to bloody revolutions, others changing the way we live, yet others simply fizzling out, relegated to the archives of history and the memory of those who experienced first hand a situation that led to a dead end street and the supremacy of a status quo. A status quo that has been beneficial for some, and harmful for others.

While my previous book may have left scars, this time I am much less concerned about being singled out by the clusters of flat-earthers, fanatics, conspiracy theorists, populists, or the corrupt. Moreover, this time there will be successful criminals who may not even realize they are such. Perhaps those who feel alluded to in some way do not even have the mental enlightenment to accept the damage they have caused to society.

To those readers who feel alluded to, ill at ease, or cannot find a comfortable position in which to sit when they read the pages of this book, I ask a thousand-and-one pardons in advance. Each paragraph has been written with love, to share ideas and reflections on social situations that affect us all in some way.

Without a doubt, it would have been much easier to sit down to write about issues that do not create controversy (fewer and fewer topics fall within this category at a time when we are overwhelmed by esoteric and conspiracy theories), or that do not contradict the opinions of people I care about. I do not believe that the quality and good intentions of a human being are defined by a simple point of view or a position taken in a debate. Nor does critical thinking make us good people.

I will be honest with you, and with myself (which means we're already getting off to a bad start): It would probably have been easier to write a book with greater sales potential, focused on some other topic. Perhaps a book of magic, or the secret formula for winning the lottery (in which, of course, everything coincides and everything contradicts itself, so that no matter what number wins, I can tell the reader "I told you so!"). It would be much more interesting to see the kind of reception readers give a book like this. Or even a wonderful self-help book to change your destiny, manipulate love, or earn money without working (naturally written by the famous writer who got rich writing and lecturing on how to get rich doing nothing).

It would also have been easier to write and sell a book about hope, faith and joy, rather than about a hard and uncertain future in a complex world ruled by messy, unpredictable, cruel and ruthless chance. Chance that we try to manipulate tirelessly throughout our lives, but over which we have no control. It is amazing that we even try to negotiate with chance. The lengths we go to in searching for the perfect way to understand chance are impressive. We have dared to name it, communicate with it, and even try to find a way to influence it or put it in favor of our desires. However, the relationship between chance and our psyche does not seem random. It is the product of millennia of evolution. The feeling of being able to influence chance lowers our anxiety and introduces optimism, which in turn translates into an evolutionary advantage and behavior that adapts more easily to changes in the environment. Discovering that there is much to know, to understand and to discover can give us a sense of freedom, but also of desolation.

It would be a mistake to think that luck can be altered, that a deceased ancestor (for example) can help us win the lottery or change our destiny. Such a conviction that chance can be controlled makes reality inaccessible to rational effort, and it is precisely rational effort that allows us to debate. It is the same rational effort that trains our minds for useful work or simply invites us to expand our knowledge, in contrast to the world of movies and novels we normally live in, full of fantasies and wonderful stories.

The name of this book could be taken as a call to violence, to hatred against gringos, banks, Russians, Chinese, immigrants, or as the preamble to a visceral discourse against businessmen, communists, United Nations conspiracies, subsidies, corruption, religion, terrorists or any other type of individual or group of individuals. I regret to inform you that this is not the line of thought you will find in this book. In fact, I hope you find just the opposite: I hope you find elements of objective reflection on the mechanisms of change in human societies.

Surely, we all dream of the day when the whole town revolts and goes out to protest with torches in front of the house of _____, looking to tear down _____, and put an end to _____ and start the road to… what? Which will lead to a new…what? Or more of… what?

In the end, if we think about it, we notice that it is easier to choose who or what to protest against than to agree on the order or system that will replace it. What exactly do we want? A new economic order? Is this viable? Do we clamor to instate something if we don't know whether it is better or viable?

It will always be easier to start a revolution against something or someone that bothers us than to actually seek meaningful change or ponder the circumstances that led to the situation in the first place.

In any case, the waves that arrive on the beach will never be static, just as our planet will continue its journey through the vastness of space, and humanity will continue its process of transformation, until the moment we are no longer here as a species.

Meanwhile, it is only a matter of time. There is nothing left but to sit back and watch the changes that lead to the next big "REVOLUTION."

Chapter 2:
What Is a Revolution?

"In politics, stupidity is not a handicap…"
— Napoleon Bonaparte

Going out to gather or hunt for food? Eating raw meat? Paying taxes to an absolute ruler who gives us no voice or vote? Riding horseback to work in the morning? Lighting a candle at night to read? Being forced to leave the house and go to an office, the only place in town where messages can be sent to other places around the country? Having to go to the library to review books, since it is the only storehouse of knowledge? All of these situations now sound meaningless and even cause us to laugh just thinking about them. But…it hasn't always been the way it is today. At some point, each of these situations was normal in the daily life of some human being.

When we think of revolutions, the guillotine often comes to mind, or crowds throwing Molotov cocktails, civil wars, bloodbaths or coups, in a fierce struggle for power. All of this is true, but only to a certain extent. Revolutions are not always like that. The term "revolution" encompasses much more than just the struggle for power. It implies changes in the lifestyle of ordinary people like you or me. It is true that there are revolutions with political connotations, but in the same way, there will be revolutions not directly related to politics. Others will have scientific connotations. Some will be violent, others will be peaceful, some will have economic implications, others will simply bring changes in the way we live and in our culture at a given time. There will be revolutions that change our lives forever, leading us along a path from which there is often no turning back.

At other times, things happen that lead us to believe we are on the verge of some great change, but for various reasons the change does not materialize and the status quo is maintained.

Anyway...it appears that not all forms of violence turn into revolutions, nor must all revolutions be accompanied by violence.

In the previous chapter, I mentioned something that intrigues me: What occurs in human relations that gives birth to social change? Why do these changes take hold in certain situations and not in others? What causes these changes?

Chance is our eternal companion. We will always find it sticking its nose into everything (mainly where it is not wanted) and having its way in all kinds of life situations that are none of its business. But chance alone is not able to connect human beings and generate violence, nor indicate the direction that change will follow. Changes also occur because of people themselves. People who have needs, who have feelings, and who often think. These people obey a human social structure, with all the characteristics intrinsic to our species.

As a political scientist, it is impossible for me to separate human behavior from the dynamics of power. And such power dynamics, which accompany revolutions, are composed of a whole world of complex interactions worthy of observation, study and analysis.

I remember that during a presentation of my previous book, an interesting and enriching debate took place. One of the participants in the debate insistently asked the question, "But why power?" That question kept bouncing around in my head. It reminded me of a lot of other times when I have heard questions like, "But, why do you want that?" Or, "What do you want to go there for?" Or, "What is the purpose of such-and-such?" Simple: the fact that something does not please one person, or does not have value for one person, does not mean that it does not exist or have value for another person. Power is a value for those who dedicate their life to fighting for it, and whether we like it or not, it is the backbone of order and in many respects defines our social structure. Power is at play in multiple social aspects, ranging from the economy and political decisions to the ability to influence the behavior of a segment of the population.

The word "revolution" has a Latin origin. It comes from the word revolutio, which means to rotate, revolve, or turn. The word originally referred to changes in the foundation of political power. According to the sciences of evil (a.k.a. the political sciences), the word implies a revolt that challenges and replaces the dominant group in society, whether economic, intellectual or political. Such shifts in the dominant power within our societies are part of the history of human civilization. They have accompanied us over the millennia, whenever we have felt the desire for something to change, or for something that might change to remain the same.

The struggle for resources is a characteristic of our species and of any other society of living beings. So what makes revolutions different? Why do they vary in duration, method, degree of violence, or even their ideological underpinnings?

Frequently, revolutions start brewing under oppressive systems that do not allow for significant participation or are not perceived as equitable. As expected, they occur more easily when there is inflexibility in the social structure or problems in the control institutions, particularly when the institutions are inoperative, ineffective or inefficient.

The motivations are not always the same. While it is true that a despot can be removed from power by a people thirsty for justice and balanced institutions, it is also true that the removal of a despot can be incredibly attractive to another power-hungry individual hoping to become the new despot. (Unfortunately, public speaking and theatrical performance are excellent and often inseparable friends, making it easier for charismatic types to deceive their audience.) In other words, all the effort poured into a revolutionary process often ends up merely replacing one imperfect system with another social order with flaws of its own.

It is interesting to note that revolutions, whether formal or informal, can involve anger and frustration. These feelings lead to what is called social behavior, cancelling out the capability of rational thinking. Ideology, per se, rarely seems to be a revolutionary engine.

Revolutions produce a sudden transformation in the center of social control by moving control from one group to another, or from one social class to another. They involve changes in ideas and/or beliefs. Many times, they even transform social values. A good example of revolution with transformation of social values was the revolution carried out by Jesus of Nazareth within Judaism, offering a different way of understanding man, his environment, and the divine. But such a change would not have been complete without the organization of a movement and the transformation of previously existing institutions.

The great revolutions that generate profound changes in social institutions often require the formation of formally or informally organized social movements. A social movement is nothing more than a group of people that organizes and empowers the weakest part of the population to be more effective in challenging elites within the social system. Of course, it could easily be said that a revolt, by itself, leads to nothing. What marks a before and after is the organization and structure of the protesters with regard to what needs to be done, why it needs to be done, what they hope to accomplish, how they plan to accomplish it, and what will happen once the dominant social structure has been toppled.

The absence of an organization to guide the process can lead to a loss of control and a period of confusion and uncertainty. This power vacuum can result in terrible anarchy, which can spread with often unimaginable consequences in the absence of authority and order.

There are authors who suggest that virtually the only reason revolutions arise is to do away with a particular class or a certain dominant social group. I don't share that point of view. As mentioned before, the resentful majority chafes at being dominated by a minority (not realizing, perhaps, that that's the way it's always been and always will be, or perhaps they harbor the hope that a revolution will elevate them to membership in the jet set). The situation is exacerbated by the fact that the majority is given little opportunity to participate, is ignored, or has perceived that the minority has little intention of taking them into account when decisions are made.

Everywhere you look, there are discontented individuals who think that perhaps they are the only ones to be so unhappy with a particular situation. Suddenly, someone says, "I don't like this." Or "That doesn't seem right to me." Or more commonly, "Those SOBs...who do they think they are?" And that's where it all begins. Then someone else says, "Aha! Just as I suspected... now I know I'm not alone. There's someone else who shares my frustration," and they start talking.

And what happens when two people talk? Of course, a third person tries to listen in on the conversation, secretly. Later, in other company, he may comment, "it's rumored that... ." (It's easier to say, "People say that" than to say "I think that…" or "It's my opinion that… .") For a fourth malcontent, the words "they say that…"

provide the impetus for what will become a snowball, with a high risk of turning into an avalanche.

Hence, the importance of the media. Traditional media is able to control the start of gossip and even allows gossip to be created at the convenience of the editorial line, or of the economic, political or social group that controls the medium.

Then, from the gossip, or rumor, or "news" (however you prefer to call it; in the end, there may not be much difference between the terms), malignant creativity appears. This is precisely the moment when someone comes up with the great idea of "Why don't we do something...?" and tells their idea to someone with initiative (also malicious).

Then the gossip or rumor, which reached the creative who forwarded it to the one with initiative, continues its upward spiral, when the one with initiative sends it along to another with previous experience and some knowledge. And that knowledge, precisely that knowledge, is what we are most interested in examining in this book.

The issue is that this comment-turned-rumor, turned inspiration for the creative, turned substrate for the one with initiative, turned impulse for the one with experience, finally transforms into protests. There are different ways of protesting, such as closing streets, rallies, marches, picket lines, etc. (Today the list includes tweets, information chains and posts on social networks —from the comfort of our sofa, of course, in front of the TV in the living room).

The thing is that protests (I mean the real ones, not the tweeting that forms part of our daily ritual of procrastination), are fragile. If it is hard for you to deal with your partner during a heated discussion, imagine what it is like to deal with dozens...hundreds... thousands...of enraged people, feeding off each other's frustration, anger, and discontent with respect to the comment-turned-rumor made by that individual a few days before.

Crowds are usually angry and subject to stress. Stress from their own anger, stress from the uncertainty (of not knowing how the group that controls power will respond—which will probably be in a violent or less-than-friendly way), and stress from not knowing what the stress and anger of the rest of the multitude will lead to.

Multiple scholars have dedicated themselves to understanding the connection between individuals within a group. We know that individuals come together to share resources, knowledge, values, and—why not?—emotions. Individuals join together in dynamic groups in which similar values are shared, resulting in what is known as "group mind," "mass mind," or "social mind."

In 1893, Emile Durkheim introduced the term "collective consciousness" to describe the set of beliefs, ideas and attitudes shared within a group. According to the philosopher Antonio Gramsci, collective consciousness refers to a multitude of individuals forming a great unified whole. This is often seen in unions and protest groups. In any case, the framework of interests that unite them must be defined.

Within the crowd, there are always certain people who incite the group to greater anger and stress. They are what the police label as "agitators." The police usually look for and identify them from the early stages of the protest, because they know they are the ones who can induce, initiate or spread any type of violent action. It can be said that the agitators are the ones who usually cause the situation to get out of control, promoting a clash between protesters and law enforcement that can lead to that terrible first casualty. From there, the spiral of violence grows ever worse.

Once the authority learns that a mob is forming, the most appropriate course of action is to seek dialogue as a way of morally deactivating individuals identified as agitators and/or leaders within the group. This is a preventive measure that will help maintain order and avoid injuries and even deaths by thwarting violent physical confrontation. Of course, this is what an intelligent authority would do (although there are times when we are more hopeful of finding extraterrestrial intelligence). Dialogue also causes the mass to perceive a certain amount of flexibility in the authority (remember that the best fuel to ignite the mass is oppression, inflexibility and little opportunity for participation).

An inflexible and challenging attitude on the part of the authority, on the other hand, is highly likely to generate violence. And once violence erupts, control becomes more difficult, since those who must be the "guardians of order" begin to be seen as targets by the mass. These individuals who represent the authority, whose presence alone has previously instilled respect or perhaps even fear, now become the bull's eye at which the mass will direct physical violence as a way of venting their feelings of anger and frustration.

Now we are faced with what in mass psychology is called a "collective behavior." The individual conscious, with all its components, begins to dissolve within a great subconscious, the subconscious of the crowd. The jumble of individual passions and feelings against the current order will serve as an amalgam to unite the mass psychologically. The mass, formed by the connection between individuals, can make for an unstable and often unpredictable environment. It is in situations like this that we see looting, with the participation of people who we would never have imagined were capable of taking so much as a pencil lying the sidewalk.

Let's put it like this: Are you predictable when you're angry? Ok, now let's say you're very angry. Are you still predictable? If the answer is still yes, I congratulate you.

What about conditions where you are very angry but there are also two other people who are equally angry (over the same issue) next to you. Still predictable?

Perfect, now imagine yourself surrounded by tens, hundreds, thousands of people with a degree of anger comparable to yours. There will always be a threshold in the number of angry people acting together where predictability flies out the window.

So, let's return to the issue of the mob that was forming from a comment that became a rumor. A person who otherwise would not have made a peep now feels empowered, surrounded by stressed and angry people with strong shared feelings that unite them. The protests allow them to manifest en masse as they would not — and could not—have done individually.

The mass begins to revolve around the desire to defy authority, to eliminate the established order, even if it is the only thing they have in common.

Most of the time, the mass vents its collective behavior without seeing its aspirations realized. In those cases, there is only a revolt (an explosion of violent collective behavior, but without achieving substantial changes in public order or social organization), which is quickly repressed and then relegated to the long list of history's anecdotes.

Some revolts may lead to subsequent changes, with a little help from time and circumstance. An example that comes to mind is the Panamanian revolt of January 9, 1964, in which my father participated, when a group of students from Panama's National Institute marched from the school to challenge the occupation of the Panama Canal area by the United States. In the end, the revolt left about twenty-two Panamanians and four Americans dead, along with dozens of wounded. Even my maternal uncle suffered an explosive bullet wound which almost cost him a limb, despite the fact that the United States Army denied using this type of ammunition (explosive bullets were banned by the Declaration of the Hague in 1899 because of the unnecessary suffering they caused). True, the incident opened a debate leading to the negotiation of the treaty that transferred the Panama Canal to the Panamanian State, but the aspiration did not materialize until thirteen years later.

These are difficult events that hit us hard, whether they achieve change or not, and whether the changes are for the better or for the worse. There is nothing soft about this type of situation. I don't see why we should study them as part of the soft sciences, making ourselves soft in the process, rather than studying collective behavior with the meticulousness and scientific objectivity it merits.

In the next chapter, we will take a look at some revolutions that forever changed our societies and our lives.

Chapter 3:
Revolutions in History

"Great spirits have always encountered violent opposition from mediocre minds."

— Albert Einstein

Now that we know what a revolution is, we have even more reason to be concerned about the violence they can generate, as well as their effectiveness. I clearly remember a couple of girls who wanted to start a revolution and challenge the status quo in their parents' house in order to have more play time, only to earn a spanking and a scolding.

It is also interesting to see whether a revolution can be consummated effectively without violence. Perhaps the same girls in the previous paragraph would have achieved more with a hug, good grades in school, and some skillful bargaining.

Apparently, many (if not the vast majority of) revolts do not move beyond the level of dreams and fiction stories due to the lack of organization in their economic, political and/or military capacity to consolidate success.

So what exactly is a peaceful revolution? Or a non-political revolution? By definition, it would seem the terms are oxymorons. However, the concept itself deals with challenging the dominant elite. Even in peaceful revolutions, there is a replacement or modification in the makeup of the elite. Many times the elite do not even know the situation is changing, and that they will no longer have the upper hand as they did before. It was during the Agricultural Revolution, for example, that the social order began to be controlled with weapons. The Renaissance facilitated the rise of the merchant class, with particular emphasis on humanist and artistic aspects. The Enlightenment laid the groundwork for citizens to demand their rights and aspire to equality under the law (which sometimes seems to elude us even 300 years later!). The Industrial Revolution transformed and gave merchants even more power, thereby widening the gap between rich and poor.

As we can see, even when revolutions are peaceful, they imply effective changes in culture and social order, and—whether we like it or not—they have political impacts, often irreversible.

Sometimes, we are not aware that we are living in a revolution as it happens. We only see changes in the midst of uncertainty, not knowing what the future holds, some of us hoping that everything will go back to the way it was before.

In the atmosphere of uncertainty spawned by revolutions, what most abounds is speculation about the threats and opportunities that lie ahead.

Below we will take a look at some of the political revolutions that have had the greatest impacts on our lives, laying the foundations for society as we know it today.

In my previous book, *From Primates to Politicians*, I covered the Neolithic revolution, in which agriculture was introduced in human societies. So let's look at other examples of revolutions:

The Renaissance

Wait a second…that was a revolution? Well, let's look at the facts, and you can judge for yourself.

The fall of the Roman Empire marked the beginning of the Middle Ages, also known as the Dark Ages of Western Europe. During this period much of the knowledge, humanism and developments achieved in antiquity were lost.

The Renaissance was a period between the 1300s and 1600s when a cultural, political, scientific and intellectual flourishing spread across Europe. It was during this period that the knowledge that had been forgotten during the Dark Ages was rediscovered.

It all started with the spread of the bubonic or black plague, which brought a migratory wave of survivors to Western Europe. Riding on this wave, the epidemic spread throughout the continent, altering all of the demographic, economic, political and cultural dynamics in its path. (Perhaps it has never occurred to us to consider the "bubonic revolution" or the "pestilent revolution." But that's okay, since it wasn't in fact a revolution because the changes were not organized or executed consciously by human beings, but were merely biological circumstances.) It is estimated that the epidemic wiped out between 30 and 60 percent of the population of Europe between 1346-1361. Bubonic plague is a highly contagious disease caused by a bacterium (Yersinia pestis) and transmitted by the fleas of rats. The bacteria are also transmitted by contact with fluids of infected patients or corpses. It is thought to have begun as a mutation in a bacterium present in Asia, which then spread until it became a true pandemic.

The migratory wave continued, increasing again with the fall of Constantinople in 1493 at the hands of the Turks. With this, the last bastion of classical Greek knowledge of the Eastern Roman Empire collapsed.

Migrants from Eastern Europe brought knowledge of classical arts and philosophy to Western Europe, as well as mastery of the Greek language (which allowed them to understand and translate the original classics). This sparked the interest of Western Europeans, who by then had lost much of their cultural and intellectual baggage. Popular wisdom starts to rouse, realizing that it had been submerged in obscurity (well, there are still people today immersed in darkness, but usually, those who live in such gloom don't even realize it).

Some also argue that there was a wave of migration of academics fleeing the conflict between the Spanish Catholic kings and the Moors, and that many of them migrated to what is now Italy (the Moors had maintained their interest in mathematics and astronomy throughout the Dark Ages).

The Renaissance was an avalanche of knowledge that converged in what is now Italy. It paved the road for a full-blown cultural revolution, with an explosion in exploration, commerce, and even in wars.

As always, there are those who identify opportunities where most see only changes. There were families of merchants such as the Medici who took advantage and increased their wealth. The Medici were funders of artists who claimed a sort of return to the greatness of ancient Rome. Today, it would be as strange as taking advantage of a migratory wave to say "make Rome great again."

The death of prominent people in the commercial and political sphere quickly opened up new opportunities for plague survivors (there's always the possibility of ascent within a company upon the demise of the immediate boss). There are academics who indicate that this increase in "social mobility" (a concept I will touch on later in this book) was a crucial factor for the movement of commerce and the development of innovation. It was, in other words, a bloody revolution, with a massive death toll and the rupture of the existing elite. The difference was that the deaths and damage to the elite were caused by biological and epidemiological conditions, not by human organization. Mother Nature took charge, without the aid of stones, sticks, bullets or Molotov cocktails.

The new interest in arts such as painting and sculpture in turn revived interest in the study of disciplines such as anatomy and geometry, with the development of perspective. The musical sphere featured the invention of new instruments such as the clavichord and the violin family. There was also a rapprochement between music and poetry.

We must ask ourselves, then, exactly *what* was "organized", and *which* social order did it challenge? There is one man who, if he lived today, could provide us with a detailed answer. His name: Galileo Galilei. Galilei was an astronomer and physicist, among other things. Funded by the Medici family, he proposed the mathematical challenge to the theoretical authority of Aristotle. On June 22, 1633, he was convicted of heresy for believing and upholding ideas contrary to the sacred and divine scriptures. The conviction included a ban on the publication of his book *Dialogue Concerning the Two Chief World Systems*, as well as house arrest (similar to famous businessmen after major corruption scandals, except that Galileo did not have a mansion and did have to spend the rest of his life locked up in a small space). The irony is that Galilei was defending ideas previously raised by a Polish priest, doctor, mathematician and astronomer (among other things), Nicolaus Copernicus. Copernicus demonstrated the ability to separate his scientific curiosity from his religious beliefs. He stated that the earth was not the center of the universe and that it revolved around the sun. His ideas were initially rejected by Protestants and later by the Catholic Church itself (although today nobody wants to claim the dubious "honor" of having banned, criticized or singled out Copernicus for defying the popular ignorance of the moment). Decades after the death of Copernicus, the world witnessed the death of Giordano Bruno (also known as the first martyr of modern science) at the stake, for defending Copernicus' theory. Galilei was absolved by Pope John Paul II, 359 years, four months, and nine days after his sentence (that is, almost 350 years after his death). The absolution was issued shortly after a commission appointed by the Pope himself confirmed that there was no reason to absolve, rehabilitate, or make any kind of apology.

The Renaissance was also the stage from which a member of the French nobility, René Descartes, evaded censorship. Disguising the novelty of his ideas, he laid the groundwork for modern philosophy. His focus on rationalism in the application of mathematics guides the sciences as we know them today.

Now, returning to the dissemination of classical knowledge: advances in mathematics brought new ways of managing finances, which were used to make families such as the Medicis (who would become the backers of Galileo Galilei, Michelangelo, Leonardo da Vinci and Rafael) even richer. This more technical management of finance produced a proliferation of trade, replacing feudalism. The emerging merchant class began to gain ground, occupying space formerly reserved for kings and religious leaders within the upper spheres of power. There would come a time when powerful merchant families would even instate and depose rulers and religious leaders at their convenience (not very different from what we have today). The previously established elite now had a new member who would ensure that things would never again be the same.

The recovery of classical knowledge also led to academic experimentation and heightened clashes between science and religion.

The proliferation of knowledge coincided with the introduction of the printing press by Johannes Gutenberg in 1440, which made knowledge accessible to many people who otherwise could not acquire it. Such widespread dissemination of information can perhaps only be compared to the rise of the Internet in the 1990s.

On the other hand, the large number of deaths brought to the table the debate about eternal life, the importance of earthly life, and humanism. Of course, when it is easy to die, the interest in living for the moment increases, since today, at least, is guaranteed to all.

All this led to a surge in man's attempts to dominate nature, an endeavor we continue to pursue to this day, sometimes successfully, other times not so much. The truth is that nature never stops marveling us, showing us how much we need to learn, and, of course...how fragile we are, on our little wet rock that travels through space.

The Enlightenment

If in some sense the Renaissance did not achieve its mission, it could be said that the Enlightenment was a new, slightly more organized attempt to bring knowledge and humanism to the center of social decision making. During the Enlightenment, education began to become universal, along with the proliferation of public libraries and museums (as we know them today). There are historians who see the two social phenomena as one, in which the Enlightenment was nothing more than the continuation of the scientific revolution started by the Renaissance (with its focus on the study of the tangible world).

The Enlightenment, also known as the Age of Reason, was a philosophical movement that began in

Europe during the 1600s and 1700s, and then expanded to its colonies. The enlightened were considered responsible for illuminating the intellect and human culture, with concepts such as reason, freedom and the scientific method. The enlightened were skeptical about religion, and their ideas were characterized by the structuring of thought around the scientific method and the secularization of knowledge. All this forced Western religions to revise their doctrines, while strengthening societies such as the Masons and Illuminatis.

Some great thinkers of the Enlightenment include physician John Locke; philosophers Thomas Hobbes, Jean-Jacques Rousseau, Thomas Jefferson, and Immanuel Kant; scientists such as Isaac Newton, and the father of modern conventional economic wisdom, Adam Smith.

All of them, in different ways, contributed to spreading the concept that human beings have rights and that governments cannot dictate individual conscience. They also spread the ideas of freedom we still fight for today.

Adam Smith merged the ideas of the Enlightenment with politics and economics. John Locke promoted the concept of representative government and laid the foundation for what would later become human rights. François-Marie Arouet, better known as Voltaire, promoted the concept of freedom of religion and speech and the separation of church and state. Jean-Jacques Rousseau advocated a form of democratic government (in a Europe full of despotic monarchies). Immanuel Kant laid the foundations for later philosophical currents based on rationalism and empiricism.

Without a doubt, the propagation of humanist concepts, as well as the transformation in the understanding of social, political and economic systems, were pillars that empowered citizens to openly challenge oppressive or non-participatory systems. As a tactic to avoid tensions, dissemination of these concepts occurred through a system in which censors were seen as cultural intermediaries rather than repressors.

The paradigm of the Enlightenment was that science could define, study and understand the universe created by God. It also began to perceive the vastness and movement of the universe. Rationalism was promoted as the most legitimate way of thinking, and as a vehicle to introduce improvements in human society. It was understood that only reason can lift mankind out of ignorance. Even today, reason and ignorance continue to fight for control of the human mind.

It was the period of the Enlightenment, for example, that saw an end to the witch hunts of the sixteenth and seventeenth centuries, during which hundreds of innocent men and women were hanged or burned at the stake, often for no specific reason. A struggle aimed at the destruction of paganism and heresy, in the style of *malleus maleficarum*, had evolved throughout Europe into a fierce persecution rife with atrocities in the name of justice and religion, lasting for over a century. Today, the practice of witchcraft, sorcery, magic, and spells is regarded as merely a way of scamming ingenuous and superstitious individuals, and punishable at most by a few days in jail or a fine. Ironically, as American physicist Michio Kaku has observed, if any of us were to travel to the past with our current technology, we would quickly be singled out as a magician or sorcerer. Can you imagine what it would be like for a citizen of the sixteenth century to bump into you, carrying in your hand a device that lets you to communicate with people halfway across the world and gives you access to the greater part of the information generated by mankind?

Despite the fact that the Enlightenment in itself did not change the social structure, it had the same effect as the anger-spawning rumor mentioned earlier, sparking a number of revolts. Two of these revolts were consolidated as famous revolutions: the American and the French. Meanwhile, the desire for knowledge also opened the door to the invention of new technologies, and with them, innovations that brought new business opportunities, leading to a new, silent uprising: the Industrial Revolution.

The American Revolution

The American Revolution was the consolidation of a revolt by thirteen North American colonies seeking independence from the British Empire, which they accused of tyranny. How ironic that those colonies have become the vast nation they are today, thanks to the "anti-imperialist" ideals of their Founding Fathers.

The story goes that in 1770, 2,000 British soldiers arrived in Boston to enforce *tax collection* according to British law. The colonists resisted and were suppressed. Subsequently, certain stores that sold British goods became the object of vandalism. An officer who lived near one of the stores opened fire, killing an 11-year-old boy. This ignited passions even more, leading to a confrontation between British soldiers and local workers. A few days later, another series of events caused a further escalation of violence, in what is known as the Boston Massacre. These events opened people's eyes to the abuses of the British Empire and served to undermine the relationship between the empire and its thirteen colonies, which would unite in a common cause: to defend themselves from the British. The colonies first rejected the authority of the British parliament, later expelling royal officers from their territories.

The American Revolution began in earnest in 1774 and ended in with the victory of the colonies in 1781. Order was maintained during and after the uprising thanks to the previously existing political and institutional structures in place in the autonomous governments of each of the colonies.

The ideas of the Enlightenment spread throughout the American colonies and were embodied in laws that gave more power to the people and less power to the rulers. The colonists rejected the oligarchies and advocated the development of republics based on enlightenment and liberalism. Thomas Jefferson, in particular, had a great influence on the Enlightenment and was charged with drafting the Declaration of Independence. In it, he expressed the ideas of John Locke, highlighting the concepts of freedom, equality, and human rights.

The death toll of this war for independence is estimated at around 37,000. As the first ally of the revolution, France's support was crucial. The French government supplied arms without ever suspecting that its own soil would become the epicenter of the next great revolution. France's support was secured thanks to the efforts of the colonies' first ambassador: the philosopher, scientist, Mason, and one of the greatest representatives of the Enlightenment in North America, Benjamin Franklin.

The ideals of freedom that spurred the colonies to independence were the same ones which decades later would plunge the new nation into an even bloodier conflict at a cost of 700,000 lives: the American Civil War.

The French Revolution

Some revolutions seem to start from the search for equality or an equitable system but end up giving way to authoritarian systems. Despots can see opportunity in the lack of organization of political and military structures, or they simply see farther into the future than those who fail to consider the potential consequences.

The beheading of Louis XVI and his wife Marie Antoinette during the French Revolution brought an end to the country's monarchy and opened the door to the establishment of a republic. With this, the power wielded by the nobility and the Catholic Church was handed over to the State under the motto *Liberté, Égalité, Fraternité*, and the Declaration of the Rights of Man and of the Citizen was drafted.

The revolution (1789-1799) was brutal, characterized by a reign of terror and a final death toll estimated at 40,000. It was followed by the dictatorship of Napoleon, who assumed responsibility for spreading the republican ideals of the Enlightenment through the use of force and weapons.

According to some authors, the whole thing started with an attempt by the government to ***raise taxes*** in order to cover the high fiscal deficit of a nation in precarious economic conditions (any similarity with any current scenario is sheer coincidence). Half of the state budget was earmarked to pay off debt.

To a large extent, say some historians, this debt was the result of the deflation of a huge bubble created by one of the biggest financial schemes of the eighteenth century, the Mississippi Company (*Compagnie du Mississippi*). The Mississippi Company was responsible for managing the Louisiana Territory in North America. In France, the company sold great expectations (speculation) regarding the wealth and potential of Louisiana (big dreams of gold, silver and cheap (slave) labor). In reality, however, the region was nothing more than marshland. The French government was sucked into buying all the shares it possibly could, causing the price of the stock to skyrocket. When the bubble burst, it left behind a deficit from which the government could not recover (apparently the lesson was not well learned, given that a little over a century ago the French elite found itself involved once again in a company with inflated expectations, this time related to the construction of the French Canal through the isthmus of Panama).

During the ensuing revolution, liberal groups and the common masses took to the streets to demand a new constitution. Forces loyal to the king challenged the masses (big mistake), causing an escalation in the fighting between groups. The crowds forced the king's forces to withdraw, making it easier for them to obtain weapons and gunpowder.

Storming of the Bastille by Jean-Pierre Houël

Emotions were causing French society to polarize, to the point of turning what began as a legitimate clamor into a reign of terror (there are reports that over 16,000 death sentences were handed down in just two years). This all happened spontaneously, without clear leadership, until Napoleon took virtually absolute control in 1799.

Unlike the revolution in North America, the French Revolution was neither planned nor organized. There was no clear vision for the future. There were no strong institutions on which to transfer power. There was no place for negotiation, nor was a dialogue established between the parties. It just happened.

The Industrial Revolution

It is said that there have been three industrial revolutions, with several waves within each.

The First Industrial Revolution was simply a transition from manufacturing by hand to the use of machines. Although the ancient Romans developed some degree of automation, the first machines as we know them today are attributed to the British.

James Watt is credited with converting the movement of water vapor into a rotary movement, making it useful for the development of machines. The first steam engine is attributed to Thomas Savery, in 1698. However, it was not until 1712 that the first steam piston was invented by Thomas Newcomen.

With the surge in manufacturing came mechanization, together with labor-related changes in society. It is reported that there was a decrease in the birth rate as well as a reduction in the infant mortality rate. In general, the indicators were not bad. Per capita income improved, but a huge gap also opened up between rich industrialists and poor workers.

It can be said that the Industrial Revolution sparked the debate over the generation of wealth and labor rights. Debates also emerged around socioeconomic dynamics and even around changes in social structure and societal and family values, in the face of a growing population and deplorable living conditions. The Industrial Revolution transferred wealth from agricultural production to industrial production, causing a huge exodus from the fields to the cities. Now, the peasants who worked the land wanted to participate in the Industrial Revolution and its higher standards of living, albeit immersed in poverty.

There is no consensus when it comes to taking stock of the Industrial Revolution. It was, in fact, a revolution, because it changed the structure of the social fabric, the dynamics of power, the economy, and the way we all live, for better or worse. It is even easier now for countries with greater industrial capacity to win at war, thanks to the mechanization of their production. In other words, not only did the gap widen between industrialists and workers: a gap also emerged in the power relationship between industrialized and non-industrialized nations.

A Second Industrial Revolution took place in the middle of the nineteenth century, with the use of mainly petroleum-derived chemicals as the source of energy for the machines of production. This was followed by a surge in the use of electrical energy, both for production and in homes.

Machines, electrification, and the application of knowledge in fuels were shaping a new economic order based on the development of science and technology to innovate and generate more wealth.

Industrial capacity and the concomitant generation of new technology translated into even greater competitive advantage for industrialized countries, an advantage they would not be willing to share, as demonstrated at a certain point by prohibiting the sale of machines to the non-industrialized world. This might seem strange, since today there is no need for such maneuvers. Industrialized countries now have their advantage secured through complex structures of scientific and technological resources that reduce the threat of competition by emerging countries.

On the other hand, industrialization has also paved the way for consumerism, environmental degradation, possible acceleration of climate change, and even industries with economies larger than those in many countries.

In short, whether by providing us with many of our modern comforts or by threatening environmental and social wellbeing, the industrial revolution has changed the dynamics of power and left an indelible mark on our way of life.

The Russian Revolution

In October 1917, Russia was plunged into a bloody civil war between the Bolsheviks and the White Army. The war lasted until 1921, with the triumph of the Bolsheviks and the subsequent establishment of the Union of Soviet Socialist Republics in 1923.

It all began in 1905, before the start of the First World War, with a popular uprising to demand civil rights and a parliament for the people of Russia, nothing very different from the ideas of freedom propagated in Europe during the Enlightenment. For the Tsar, a good way to maintain national unity (and remain in power) was to succeed against an external enemy, and the "Great War" (World War I) provided just such an opportunity. The strategy backfired when over 250,000 men were lost in the battle of the Masurian lakes in 1914 against opposing forces. Though the balance shifted in Russia's favor in 1916 against Austria and the Ottoman Empire, the economy was reeling from the cost of the war, including hundreds of thousands dead and millions wounded.

The battered economy triggered riots due to food shortages during the war, forcing Tsar Nicholas II to abdicate in February 1917. In his place, a Russian Provisional Government of moderate liberals and socialists was established, headed by Aleksander Kerensky, a lawyer, politician and brilliant and charismatic orator who was well versed in the parliamentary system and had a history of rivalry with the tsarist monarchy. Meanwhile, Bolshevik anarchists and agitators presented themselves as anti-war radicals.

The Bolsheviks had started as a faction of the Marxist Russian Social Democratic Labour Party. The party became divided over a book written by Lenin in 1902 in which he stated that the revolution required a leader with a hard hand who should subsequently leave power to make room for socialism, but with a distinction made between politicians and workers. This distinction was not accepted by the faction that adhered most closely to Marxism and defended the idea of a completely classless society. The Bolsheviks (derived from the Russian *bolshinstva*, which means "majority") finally separated from the party in 1912 and formed their own independent party: The Russian Social Democratic Labour Party (Bolsheviks).

The Bolsheviks led the anti-war agitators and dedicated themselves to undermining the army's capacity and promoting disobedience. They sold the idea of social transformation and an alternate formula to end the war. In other words, they focused the civil war on a class struggle, which was attractive to peasants and workers who longed for a better life. Of course, with the cost in lives, added to economic precarity, it would not have been strange had the masses of peasants begun to desert and sympathize with the enemy.

Finally, General Lavr Kornilov, the Commander-In-Chief of the Russian Army (an anti-Bolshevist of Cossack origin who was more interested in increasing the power of the army than in political ideologies), led an attempted coup that weakened Karensky's mandate and opened the way for the Bolsheviks to overthrow him in October 1917. The Central Powers (Austria-Hungary, Germany, Bulgaria and the Ottoman Empire) responded to the revolution with an armistice. However, an attack by German and Austro-Hungarian forces in February 1918 forced the Bolsheviks to sign the Brest-Litovsk Treaty in March of the same year. The anti-Bolshevik forces, which remained loyal to the allies, took up arms against the Bolsheviks. In the end, Russia was immersed in a civil war between the Bolsheviks and conservative White Army forces. As in any armed conflict, the most politically and militarily organized faction prevailed. The Whites, for the most part, gave up, died en masse, or emigrated from Russia, until the end of the war in 1921.

The consolidation of the Russian Revolution ushered in a new era in the world order, the era of a new socialism which would spread throughout much of the globe.

The Revolution of the 1960s

Armed uprisings or changes in economic dynamics are not the only kind of revolutions the world has seen.

In the 1960s, the United States and Europe were the center of a revolution that involved ecological, sexual, political, moral, and artistic issues. For the children born just after World War II, war and destruction were not simply a possibility, but a tangible reality.

In 1963, the assassination of President Kennedy marked the beginning of a series of cultural changes among young people. An "anti-establishment" counterculture emerged, first in the United Kingdom and the United States, then spreading to much of the western world. The movement gave greater importance to Civil Rights, at the same time that war was being waged in Vietnam. It became a dividing line between two generations with regard to issues like human sexuality, rights of the disabled, gay rights, interest in the environment, awareness about the impact of poverty on the world, racial discrimination, alternative forms of spirituality, respect for authority, women's rights, and the use of psychoactive substances for recreational purposes.

Scientific advances also played their part in this cultural shift. The sexual revolution, for example, gained adherents following the emergence of more effective contraceptive methods and the use of antibiotics to control sexually transmitted diseases. In this context, the idea of recreational sex was popularized, granting greater freedom to both men and women. Telecommunications technology became another ally with the rise of television.

Certain circumstances converged during this time which added momentum to the cultural changes that would transform humanity. Alternative lifestyles emerged that gave great relevance to creativity. The fear of being drafted and sent to Vietnam, along with a heightened awareness of social injustices and inequities, the Cold War, and disappointment in the way domestic and international politics were being handled, profoundly changed the philosophical outlook of young people in the space of just five years, between 1966 and 1970.

The changes occurred amid the threat of a nuclear war between the superpowers (the Cuban Missile Crisis of 1962, which made it clear that humanity was only one press of a button away from utter devastation, remains fresh in the minds of many). The logo of the Campaign for Nuclear Disarmament (CND) was adopted by the movement as a symbol of peace and love. "Make love, not war" became the new catchphrase. Simultaneously, the space race, in the framework of the Cold War, showed us just how fragile our planet is, and how insignificant we are in the vastness of the universe.

In the end, it is clear that those young people — more educated than their parents, hoping to change society – were unable to consolidate their dreams. Their insertion into politics, society, business, or even public opinion left much to be desired. The utopian vision they spread is not the world we live in, even 50 years after the massive call for equity, justice, peace and love. There have been changes in our society to this day, but with little progress. Humanity still has many obstacles to overcome to reach an ideal world. In fact, an ideal world does not look exactly the same for everyone.

In any event, the so-called revolution of the 1960s did produce some important social changes, including the insertion of women into the workforce, laws to protect victims of diseases such as HIV/AIDS, children's rights, sexual and reproductive rights, increased awareness of violence against women, and a greater number of children born outside of marriage.

Logo of the British campaign for nuclear disarmament, designed by Herald Holton. It would become the icon of peace protests in the 1960s

Are we currently living in a revolution?

Communications seem to be driving a new industrial revolution, along with the development of biomedical technology and artificial intelligence, among other technological advances of recent years. Twenty years ago, we would not have imagined a family in which each member was checking and messaging on their cell phone at dinner time, in lieu of talking to each other.

The so-called Fourth Industrial Revolution implies changes in information and knowledge occurring with such speed that they have exceeded our ability to incorporate commensurate changes in our thought patterns. It is also observed that the dissemination of scientific advances in the media has not been proportionate to their importance nor to the impact they might have on our understanding of the universe or of ourselves in our daily life.

The development of robots is occurring at a faster rate than the adjustments that need to be made in education. This could lead to difficulties in relocating displaced workers, particularly in developing countries where it is easier to import robots due to increasingly cheaper technology than to implement educational changes within their bureaucracies. All of these changes will certainly affect the elite; economic dynamics will also continue to change in the near future.

Chapter 4:
When Reality Surpasses Fiction

"Life is not fair — get used to it!"
— Charles J. Sykes, Author

Reality is the actual existence of something. Something we are able to perceive. Sometimes we understand it, sometimes not.

Imagination, on the other hand, is what our mind creates but others cannot perceive: all sorts of immaterial events and fantasies with unlimited possibility of evolving into extraordinary ideas.

The problem is that there are times when reality contains material facts capable of challenging and ridiculing the most sophisticated attempts of our imagination to create something amazing.

We have all heard, read or even experienced things that are hard to believe. Things we would have thought possible (with much difficulty) only in the realm of imagination, but were in fact true and material.

Repeatedly, I have seen public figures with shady pasts make broad and visible demonstrations of material detachment, presenting themselves as great fathers of altruism. It is not uncommon to see all sorts of gangsters making donations to nursing homes, orphanages, hospitals, charitable foundations, etc. What piques my curiosity are their motives. Are they just trying to lower their taxes? Could it be that they are truly detached from worldly pleasures, and this is what has enabled their rise to elite status in their particular "industry?" Or is this their way of compensating society for the harm they have done on the road to riches? Or maybe it is just their way of celebrating the easy money they made. Anyway...it has been said that when there are multiple points of view, the truth is usually located somewhere in the middle. In the end, these individuals turn into socially respectable types, even earning the admiration of a certain sector of society, in the style of corrupt politicians and cronies who steal from the taxpayers while expecting to be thanked for sharing part of what they have stolen.

This chapter is not about how or why revolutions occur. It's about financial cunning and slippery types. It's about moral judgment in two different corners of the same room. Or rather, it is about those incredible instances of reality that leave us wondering at the absence of revolution. What is it that anesthetizes the masses?

I can easily bring to mind the image of my godfather in the Kiwanis Club, asking for the floor to scold the other members and calling on them to express strong objection over some event that was happening in the country at the time. The truth is that I witnessed the same scene several times, and few times did I see some kind of protest materialize around the events that were generating the restlessness. It seems that people can be paralyzed by the unbelievable, or by individual hidden agendas.

The most surprising thing is that this paralysis does not occur only in civil society. We see it happen in the institutions responsible for justice as well.

Which leads me to wonder: Could it be that the shamefulness of an act is entirely dependent on the protagonists? Is it easy to declare that someone is guilty, but only depending on who it is we are talking about? Are laws nothing more than a tangle of concepts created to confuse society and give an impression of justice, while in reality impartiality and fairness are nothing more than crazy ideals populating the imagination of the naive?

I remember once hearing an Argentine criminologist say "prisons are full of failed criminals," referring to the fact that successful criminals end up in positions of power in governments and corporations. The legal section of the newspaper *El Espectador* states it another way in the article "Prisons are full of rubes, not drug traffickers."[2] According to the The Sentencing Project, a research and advocacy center based in Washington, DC, the rate of incarceration in the United States per

2   Espectador, El. "Las Cárceles Están Llenas De Jíbaros, No De Narcotraficantes." ELESPECTADOR.COM. Accessed November 15, 2020. https://www.elespectador. com/noticias/judicial/las-carceles-estan-llenas-de-jibaros-no-de-narcotraficantes/.

100,000 inhabitants is significantly higher for Blacks and Hispanics than for whites (a painful fact for me, as a Hispanic American). It is also known that the majority of foreigners in US prisons are Mexican.[3]

In other words: The skinniest dog gets all the fleas!

So, what determines the success of someone who lacks ethics? What makes them end up a bank president, or in jail?

Multiple studies that have shown that a person's appearance and physical attractiveness influence the degree of trust they inspire. We know that physically attractive students get better grades than their less comely peers, with the same amount of effort. We know that less physically attractive subjects are at greater risk of being convicted in a trial. In other words, decisions are biased, even in systems that boast of being the most equitable and fair.

It is not surprising, then, that in addition to physical appeal there are other aspects that deform the measuring rod with which people are judged, evaluated, or punished. In the years I have been working as a doctor, I have had the opportunity to attend daily to people from all social levels and conditions. I must admit that when dealing with people who have made some kind of mistake or been imprisoned for a crime, the ones who are considered high profile have a characteristically dazzling smile together with a charisma and fineness of form typical of men and women who easily gain the

---

3   "Las Cárceles De Estados Unidos, Llenas De Latinos." BBC News Mundo. BBC. Accessed November 15, 2020. http://www.bbc.com/mundo/noticias/2011/09/110907_eeuu_latinos_prision_en.

trust of society, including health professionals. The stereotypical criminal found in films is usually limited to the common, low-profile delinquent.

If you think about it, just how guilty can a person be? Well, that depends on how good his lawyers are, and how well inserted he is into the system. Of course, their financial status is also a factor, since it improves the possibility of hiring a good lawyer or having better connections.

For the most part, prisons are full of individuals from the lower social strata. What does this mean? That the upper classes have more "kosher" behaviors? That they're more ethical and inclined to good customs and morals? Or are they just regular human beings who are simply situated in a more advantageous position within the system?

An advantageous position even alters our understanding of ethics. Something as common and accepted as an army is not far removed from a street gang. In fact, it seems the only difference between the two is social approval, meaning the approval of the society or social group that benefits from its existence. This is so much so, that we easily find admirers of Pablo Escobar in Medellin, or Sinaloans sympathetic to "El Chapo" Guzman. Similarly, when the armed forces of a given society have lost legitimacy —a frequent occurrence throughout history —they are often called a "gang of thugs." With the loss of popular support, it is common for the population to accuse their security forces of criminal activity. I can remember cases where members of security forces were brought to trial for actions which, had they occurred with social approval, would have earned them the reputation of a great patriot simply performing their duty. The line that separates a serial killer from a soldier is very fine. A sniper's shots can make him a hero in an area of armed conflict, or a villain in the middle of a city in peacetime.

Speaking of judging actions, aberrations such as the struggle between capitalists and socialists come to mind. In savage capitalism, companies deliberately plunder defenseless citizens, while in carnivorous socialism, the state deliberately plunders its citizens to hand the money over to the selfsame companies or to its nouveau riche. In reality, the situation does not change much for those who are at an advantage, much less for those who continue to populate the ranks of the disadvantaged.

And what about the thin line separating free supply and demand from what can objectively be called the actions of thugs, with the trophy going to the one who learns how to infiltrate and move between the thin gaps left by the laws? It is a very blurred—in some cases invisible—line that separates the "great lord" from the common criminal. A line that is drawn with the pencil of cunning, the ability to use the laws or set them in one's favor, and a propensity to immorality within the legal limits. This line forms part of a drawing in which reality can be changed at will and tailored to size.

When we feel that there has been social harm, we need to believe that it will accompanied by a punishment of similar intensity. When the punishment exceeds the injury, it is seen as unjust and victimizes the condemned. But what happens when there is more social harm than punishment? Often, a new godfather of organized crime emerges; at other times, we simply have a new entrepreneur, politician, or just another "success story."

It is precisely because of some of these success stories that different cultures revere criminals of almost mythical stature, such as Robin Hood, for harming the most wealthy in some way. People see such crime as an epic feat, in the style of the popular Spanish saying, "A thief who steals from a thief is richly pardoned." It is the same reason why phrases such as "he stole, but he got things done" are heard in various regions of Latin America. It is the same reason why entire communities show their admiration for drug traffickers like Pablo Escobar or "El Chapo" Guzman.

Everyone talks about the good things done by good people and the bad things done by bad people, but who really decides what is good or what is bad? In the end, it all depends on who is the winner, or the beneficiary. Everyone will say how good the party was (or wasn't) depending on how much fun they had at it. The good guys are the eternal winners, but only in movies or novels. Real life is another story. In real life, it is the strongest that win. And the winner becomes the "good guy", the one who gets to tell what happened however he chooses. What is good and what is bad is so relative that it can become the subject of mockery, as it did in Goethe's *Faust*.

We live in a society that is indifferent to the fact that more tax money is spent on the development and purchase of weapons than on health and education. Doesn't it seem wrong that materials are more expensive when they are for people's health? Or that medications and medical equipment are intentionally designed to expire? Doesn't it seem criminal to spend more resources on promoting ignorance, the arms race and political cronyism, than on caring for the welfare of citizens and ensuring a better society?

Is the definition of an illegal act the inability of its perpetrators to infiltrate the law-making process? Is it not legal to sell arms to the civilian population, or to market a large number of products that have been scientifically proven repeatedly to cause health problems? Is there not a wide range of actions that harm the environment yet are still legal?

The intention of this book is not to enter into controversies that give rise to a discourse against the elite, nor to cheap populism. As I explained in my book *From Primates to Politicians*, the existence of elites (regardless of their ideology) is part of nature. There have always been those who generate wealth through ingenuity, talent and work. It is not a sin to contribute one's talents to society, nor can it be deemed wrong to benefit from them. Everything considered, however, it is not surprising that Western politics have gradually shifted to the left. In a system that seems designed to keep the weakest down, there are many who feel their only hope lies in challenging the status quo.

The goal here is to explore the mechanisms and tricks used by the few to take advantage of the law, regardless of harming others with impunity.

Every year there are reports of thousands of fraudulent actions by white-collar criminals in virtually every country in the world. While these actions often go undetected, they always imply a financial injury (or some other type) to someone else.

According to Nobel laureate Gary Becker, white-collar criminals are not mentally ill. They simply weigh costs and benefits differently from other people (that is, they know they have a high probability of going unpunished), and often show no remorse.

Following are some examples of such actions. While not crimes per se, they are hard-to-believe acts done by allegedly honorable and successful people. All are worthy of any society magazine cover.

Stereotype of the white collar criminal

The super-banker

The super-banker was introduced into the upper echelons of power through his marriage to a lady of high society.

At one point, a newspaper from another country called him "the greatest unpunished white-collar criminal" of his country. Others call him "one of the great exploiters of the public treasury."

He has also been implicated in large land deals and real estate projects.

Nevertheless, the guy has had an impressive career. He has served as director of the national bank of his country, the social security system, the main telecommunications company, one of the main energy generation and transmission companies, and finally, the chief state-owned company. In other words, he is a person who is clear about where the money and power lie, and knows how to get there. Like any good connoisseur of politics and interpersonal relationships, he has also been involved with various foundations that allow him to whitewash his image, presenting himself as a philanthropist who cares about others.

His most outstanding achievement was evading more than $400 million (according to some experts) in taxes on the proceeds from the sale of a bank he directed for twenty years.

The uncle of this super-banker, who served as minister of economy and finance and then as comptroller, encouraged the legislature to push for a law that would legitimize the non-payment of such taxes around the time it was projected the bank would be sold. The law modified the tax rate payable on the sale of shares held for less than twenty-four months and lowered the tax rate on earnings.

The super-banker's uncle supported the bill and promoted its approval, stressing the urgency of it (it wasn't until later that everyone would find out what the real urgency was).

It was the perfect setup. The super-banker had a minister for uncle (the one who spoke in the legislature), while his main partner (and father-in-law) was uncle to the country's vice president. Incidentally, the vice president of the country was also a partner of the bank that would be sold. In fact, the latter traveled to the country of the potential buyer as a public official (all expenses paid by the government that he presided over).

The president of the country then ratified the law without a hitch and...bingo! Now the whole plot was perfectly legal. Time to proceed with the sale, with the assistance of a tailor-made law designed to suit the family needs of the super-banker. Brilliant!

Subsequently, the super-banker became minister of economy and finance in the administration led by the party that had opposed the party that sponsored the $400 million evasion. The president who appointed him was his friend and partner, and had previously denounced him for declaring his monthly income to be one dollar. During his time as minister, he was apparently involved in cases of misappropriation of funds and irregular contracts in a program closely tied to the presidency. In one instance, he defended his innocence by arguing that he had signed the contract without reading it.

At some point a millionaire died and left a fortune of $50 million, including land valued at $40 million, as an "inheritance to feed poor children." The widow engaged in a fierce legal battle with the lawyer in charge of enforcing the will and finally managed to have three court magistrates (all closely linked to political parties) annul the will and rule in her favor (of course, the poor children had no acquaintances or connections in the upper circles). When it came time to develop the land, the cunning widow sought the best possible partner: the super-banker (who was minister of economy and finance at the time). To make things even more interesting, the new partnership is laying claim to the adjacent beach (although legally, beaches cannot be allocated).

In an interview with a foreign journalist, the super-banker claimed that he had nothing to do with the change in the law, and that the taxes on the sale of the bank could have been avoided even without changing the law. Just as his partner (who had appointed him minister) had done, without anyone "making a fuss."

Since the super-banker is not stupid, he was one of the major backers of the candidate who would win the next presidential elections (not a member of the party that facilitated the evasion of taxes on the sale of the bank, nor of the one that appointed him minister). Obviously, the man knows how the game is played.

Subsequently, he has collaborated with the richest man in his country to develop homes that go for anywhere from 600,000 and more than $1 million each (among many other projects).

The evasion of taxes on the sale of the bank was criticized in newspapers and by certain not-so-popular groups, who demanded that charges be filed with regard to the corruption of public servants and the traffic of influence. Obviously, such accusations against someone so "honorable" (that is, so well connected and influential) were unacceptable. The case was never investigated and no charges were ever filed.

The super-banker also had political aspirations. That didn't go so well, but, as the Linkin Park's song goes: "in the end it really doesn't matter."

This section of the book is not narrated in bad faith. Rather, it is offered as an example. This guy could just as easily be admired for his exploits. After all, the road to some of his achievements would easily have landed any mortal being like you or me in jail.

The ghost bridge

The ghost bridge is a pile of old scrap metal lying around in a certain country.

The country where it was going to be built breached the contract it had signed with a foreign construction company. That breach of contract led to a lawsuit and subsequent conviction. The sentence required the country to pay $25 million to the construction company. The company says it will hand over the scrap metal once the compensation is paid.

The contract was for $100 million. The country where it was going to be built paid $30 million, but three years after signing, it ordered work to cease amid accusations of embezzlement of public funds at the hands of the administration in office at the time. The construction company then filed legal remedies which led to sixteen years of litigation. The case was taken to the industrial union in the country of construction, claiming $148 million in compensation.

Rumor has it that the finance minister at the time of the contract took (for personal use) part (at least) of the money for the construction, and that is why the contract could not be fulfilled. It's been said that altogether, $8 million were divvied up among the leaders of the party in power.

Eleven years after the scandal, the former minister of finance implicated in this embezzlement of public funds became president. When asked about the option of renegotiating the contract to avoid paying reparations, he replied that he would not renegotiate because the issue brought him very bad memories. In the first year of his term as president, the courts exempted him from all responsibility.

In the end, all possible participants in the multi-million-dollar embezzlement that put an end to the bridge project were investigated, but no one was found guilty.

Twenty-three years later, the former minister of finance (in office at the time of the contract), blamed the then president of the country for not approving the $60 million needed to complete the construction, claiming that the bridge was almost finished in the country of the contractor.

Naturally, the former minister linked to the scandal is a greatly respected member of high society who still exercises a certain degree of political and commercial influence in his country.

The syrup of death

The syrup of death was administered to the population by the government health system. In the span of two months, the 200,000 bottles dispensed adversely affected about 1,300 individuals, with an estimated 400 to 800 deaths. Two years later, there were estimates that the total number of people poisoned could be as high as 6,000.

The syrup of death had a surprise component which should not have been there. In fact, in the medical world, it is remembered as the greatest intoxication with a "surprise component" in the history of the world.

It took a lot of detective work to determine that the sick and dead were victims of the death syrup with its surprise component. The minister of health was even trying to blame the deaths on another medication that held no candle at the funeral. What's worse, the health minister himself was distributing the aforementioned syrup to hard-to-reach communities, meaning that there are probably additional deaths that were never included in the statistics.

The World Health Organization was asked to take part in the investigation into the cause of so many sick and dead; everyone was looking like crazy for the culprit. Finally, it was determined that the symptoms were due to poisoning. Subsequently, the surprise component was identified in the syrup prepared by the public health system, where no quality control was practiced.

The surprise component came in nine tons of contaminated and imported raw material purchased three years before the poisoning was detected. Initially, twenty-seven people were charged in the country where this "mass murder" occurred. Shortly after, the number dropped to eleven. Then a businessman and four public officials were convicted. Then, one of the sentences was extended, and two more people were convicted. To the survivors of the poisoning it seemed like very little, and twelve years later they began to demand $6 million of compensation for each one of them.

The litigation crossed borders. There were trials in the country where the poisoning occurred, in the country of the intermediary company that made the sale, and in the country of origin of the contaminated raw material (where capital punishment was even applied to two senior officials deemed responsible).

On top of all this, some leaked communications indicated that a certain "X," a person with a notorious trajectory of misdeeds and incompetence, was involved in altering the labels on the imported substance. The assertion, made by a foreign embassy official, is allegedly based on a series of documents that never came to light. "X" was listed as treasurer and president of an import company. In fact, this same individual had been previously linked to the importation of contaminated food. So why did "X" not appear on the list of those imputed, indicted or convicted? Well, this is where it gets interesting. "X" was the son of a minister of the government in power at the time of the poisoning. Naturally, "X" has argued that any finger pointing is nothing more than a political attack or mudslinging campaign against his family.

What stands out about this example is not the possible material gain in the purchase and sale of the contaminated raw material, but the ability of someone linked to such a horrific blunder to come through unscathed.

The construction bribery

Everything is so relative and circumstantial these days that it's almost laughable (as in, laughing to keep from crying) to think that Galileo Galilei spent the last nine years of his life under house arrest for divulging his scientific findings. The president of the banknote builders received a similar sentence for creating what came to be called "the largest global corruption scandal in modern history" by CNN, having paid out $788 million in bribes over a twelve-year period.

The result was a transnational legal battle in which prosecutors from multiple countries had to work together to unravel the tangle of corruption linking the company, banks, intermediary companies, corporations and corrupt politicians. But...something strange occurred. It seems that the only players to be found guilty and convicted are all intermediate or low-level businessmen and high-profile politicians defeated at the polls. In other words, those who were at a disadvantage when the scandal erupted.

Excuses were offered, such as the fear that lost jobs, financial instability, or political unrest would leave the affected countries in a state of total chaos and ungovernability. Together, they formed an impenetrable shell that protected the best-placed individuals in every country stained by the scandal, while the only legal action taken was against enemies of the dominant elite.

The result of this scandal has been the adoption by several governments of official positions protecting the company in order to prevent job losses and financial collapse in their countries.

What has yet to be explained to me is: The financial collapse of what or whom? Of the company? Of the collaborators? Of the State? Or...how about...of those who were involved but came through unscathed and continue to occupy positions of power?

In the end, as they always say, in finance and politics, those who crash, crash alone.

If there is a lesson we can take away from this, it might be that if you are going to solicit or receive bribes, first make sure that you or your close friends are elected in the next elections, so that you're spared the need to make an appearance in a courtroom or jail cell.

The white-haired president and the dilemma of "Is it or isn't it?"

One of my favorite cases is that of the white-haired president. This great teacher brought many older citizens out of their cocoon of naivety. He made them realize that they had been deceived all their lives, and that "sex" is a relative term.

The forty-nine-year-old president had already been sued for sexual harassment while holding another elected position. But this time, he had an extramarital relationship with a presidential employee, twenty-two years old.

The twenty-two-year-old employee entrusted her intimacies to a friend, who delivered the goods to an independent counselor investigating other scandals related to the white-haired president. Word spread, reaching the media, and the affair finally made it to parliament, where the white-haired president was eventually exonerated of all charges.

The white-haired president flatly denied having "sex with that woman" (referring to the twenty-two-year-old employee).

The debate heated up when it was taken to the medical sphere. It was important to determine if the white-haired president had lied, or if he had obstructed justice to cover his guilt.

The crux of the matter lay in the definition of "sex" submitted for the trial. The white-haired president argued that he had had no contact with the twenty-two-year-old employee that fit that definition. In other words, having "sexual intercourse" included the active form, but not the passive.

Finally, the white-haired president admitted having an "inappropriate physical relationship" with the twenty-two-year-old employee. It's just that what that involved did not fit the definition given in the trial.

The court sentenced him to pay a fine and restricted the exercise of his profession for five years. But there was no noticeable difference. He remained president, the fine imposed represented less than a fifth of his annual income, and the white-haired president continues to be an honorable gentleman of the nobility. In addition, he has the satisfaction of having educated the general population regarding the definitions of romance and affairs of the heart.

The energy company

The energy company had exponential growth in its early years. It became admired in the business world for its installations, and achieved a ranking among the 100 best employers in the country.

The genius of the company was to take unusual products to the stock market and offer them as "commodities"…until word got around that it paid bribes in banana republics.

Manipulation of the company's shady accounting made it the biggest business fraud in the country's history. The income reported by the corporation actually came from business dealings with its subsidiaries, hiding huge losses and a growing debt behind the doctored numbers. Indirectly, this manipulation of the company's books produced a manipulation in the value of its shares. Business probably hadn't gone as expected, so they decided to go into debt in order to bet on new initiatives that would generate the expected profits. The idea did not work.

The company went under, not the first time, but the second time it committed the same misdeed (and shortly after being named the "Energy Company of the Year" and then "the nation's most innovative company").

The general manager and intellectual author of the fraudulent accounting was recently released from prison (at the time of writing this book), after twelve years behind bars. But even today, the public continues to pay the price for the energy company's collapse, which cost investors billions of dollars and left thousands without jobs.

What stands out most in all this is not the energy company's scheme, but the fact that several business writers have stated that nothing of what happened is newsworthy. In the world of large corporations, what happened is simply "business as usual." In the end, the general manager of the energy company was not viewed as a great lord, but as a criminal. A criminal who carries with him the story of many other great lords that never had the pleasure of spending time behind bars, like the brothers in the next tale.

The collapsed conglomerate

The bankruptcy case of the "ABC" group was closed by prescription following twelve years of litigation.

This occurred after the owners, two brothers from a very prominent family, were sentenced to sixty-six months in jail for forgery and fraud. Following the conviction, the defense team filed no fewer than twenty appeals to keep the brothers out of jail. A plethora of lawyers with a history of defending white collar criminals participated in the process.

A series of irregularities in the books of the erstwhile thriving business group was topped off by a sudden bankruptcy, arousing suspicions in the financial sector. The bankruptcy became the greatest default on bank loans to date in the nation's history, spurring creditors to sue the brothers for fraud and forgery of documents. In the span of three months, the liabilities had gone from $4.5 to $26 million with no visible explanation. The brothers attributed the change in the financial statements to a series of investments that did not prosper. The truth was that the financial statements had been "adjusted" to the tune of $51 million, enabling the brothers to defraud multiple banks and other lenders. Subsequently, an apparent, unexplained "disappearance" of $54 million was detected.

In the end, since the brothers live in a banana republic, they did not serve time behind bars like the general manager of the energy company. The case ended up doing more damage to the reputation of the country's judges and magistrates than to its financial security.

The Tycoon

It is not uncommon for a millionaire to become president of a country, much less so when the laws are designed to benefit the wealthy. While this anecdote is about one person in particular, it reflects a widespread reality, illustrating the web of corruption found in multiple countries around the world.

The tycoon had a first-class financial education, which led to the acquisition of his first business while serving as a bank officer. The business grew until it became the largest in the region, enabling him to amass a fortune. He gave further proof of his mastery of the arts of finance by marrying a woman from one of the country's most respected families in social and business circles.

As a friend to every president and every political party to reach office, regardless of ideology or political current, he occupied high-profile public positions that moved contracts worth millions. All of this served to give him a clear vision of the movements of money within the country.

Of course, when a tycoon has dedicated his life to working hard to enjoy the jingle of the coins in his pocket, public service is not exactly regarded as charity work.

The tycoon decided to create his own political party and run in the next elections, which he knew he would lose (in fact, he lost with less than 6 percent of the vote). But this would help to make him known and be considered as a presidential candidate. Five years later and with more political experience under his belt, he again ran for president, capitalizing on the mistakes of previous governments, which he knew inside and out. He won by an overwhelming majority. At the time of his victory, *The Economist* estimated that the tycoon had a business network valued at least at one billion dollars.

The tycoon assumed the presidency of the country with the "Robber Barons" code of ethics under his arm, and quickly established an authoritarian, populist, and clientelist style of government. This made it much easier to conduct all kinds of business while showing his most generous side to the poor. As every scholar of politics knows, the best way to do business freely in a government is to disarm the institutions of control, which creates a power vacuum that is usually filled by a dictator, strongman or authoritarian president. Authoritarianism is usually accompanied by populism, in which "enemies of the people" are created and a propaganda campaign is unleashed to emphasize the authoritarian leader's benevolence towards the "great masses of the oppressed." This Machiavellian plan could not fail, much less so when resorting to blackmail and bribery of low-profile political opponents to achieve a majority in Congress. Such was the reach of its tentacles that the Supreme Court of Justice was brought to its knees and the attorney general was dismissed.

As expected, the government was pelted with accusations of human rights violations (including the death of street protesters), political espionage, bribery, embezzlement, money laundering, abuse of authority, and nepotism, among many other allegations by the national and international media.

The tycoon's party lost the next elections to an opponent who promised to investigate all of the irregularities committed in the tycoon's government. "To jail! To jail! Send the tycoon to jail!" was the chant that reverberated in the demonstrations organized by his adversaries, begging the new government to prosecute the abuses to the fullest extent of the law.

And indeed, it began to look like a real witch hunt. An unprecedented number of case files were opened. Incredible plots were unearthed, enough to fill several volumes of business literature. Family members, children, friends, business partners, acquaintances, company employees...all were involved to one degree or another. It seemed that during the tycoon's government, there was no clear dividing line between business dealings and criminal dealings. Such practices could easily serve as an objective definition of what popular wisdom understands as "kleptocracy" or "savage capitalism."

After a long extradition process, the tycoon was sent back to his country to face his commercial and political adversaries, who were enthusiastically wrapping the case with the flag of the "certainty of punishment" so necessary for the strengthening of the country's badly injured institutions.

So far, this doesn't sound like anything out of the ordinary for a corrupt system. The amazing thing is that of all the possible charges, the only one for which a reasonably well-documented file was compiled was "phone espionage" (reminding me a lot of the charge of "tax evasion" brought against Al Capone).

However, after assembling a team of at least twelve lawyers of the highest profile and boldest trajectories imaginable, the tycoon was released and acquitted by judges with questionable conflicts of interest. Today, the tycoon has been absolved of all sin and dwells among us.

In case you're still wondering whether this story deserves mention in this chapter on reality surpassing fiction, there's an epilogue. A working group of the Human Rights Council of the United Nations has issued a document stating that it considers the tycoon's detention to have been arbitrary, and urges his country's government to compensate him in accordance with international law.

Even more impressive is the fact that he is not the first —nor will he be the last —wealthy detainee who manages to slip through the fingers of justice, only to return to claim his rights in what seems more a mockery of collective intelligence than a demonstration of equal opportunity within society.

The petroleum republic and Commander Red Beret

The petroleum republic had been subjected to forty years of the same political practices. The country's three political parties were downsized to two, which then joined in a common law marriage, agreeing to share power and split the oil revenues between them.

Of course, the now-wealthy upper ranks of both parties (thanks to the use of their political power to divvy up the oil) became a closed and exclusive circle, with markedly unparticipatory governments.

As they say, in a democracy it is the majority that rules. The two exclusive parties had lost their sway over the majority, the same majority that would vote for Commander Red Beret.

Commander Red Beret had the gift of gab. He could talk for hours on all kinds of topics, jumping from one to another without any logical connection. But he was certainly entertaining to listen to! A one-man audiovisual spectacle! It was the kind of rhetoric only found among the great populist speakers of history. Such was his loquacity that another head of state publicly asked him to shut up (in a manner reminiscent of Kiko from the Mexican sitcom *El Chavo del Ocho*).

Between the gab and the discontent, Commander Red Beret managed to carry out multiple reforms in social policies, in international politics, and in the country's constitution. He even explored the fabric of the geopolitical game.

In the end, he was able to hold on to power and get himself re-elected until the day of his death, to be followed by his hand-picked successor.

So what is the lesson here?

Well, the lesson was not provided to us by Commander Red Beret, but by his daughter, who says she amassed a fortune of over $4 billion (according to a prestigious business magazine) thanks to honest work, good savings habits and the virtually door-to-door sale of a certain brand of creams and cosmetics. Naturally, under the government of her father's anointed, there is no judicial raising of eyebrows over the unusual fortune.

From all this, we can conclude that if you're in the business of selling creams, be sure to use them on yourself, because one of them just might turn out to be the formula for good fortune!

According to Transparency International, oil wealth often remains in the hands of industry-related politicians and businessmen, in conditions that do not disclose profits, payments, or final beneficiaries. These conditions are perfect for corruption schemes.

The bomb cities

Perhaps few events in the history of mankind produce as much emotion as seeing photos or footage of the debris left behind in the bomb cities.

You might even call it the cherry on top of the impunity sundae.

A blinding light illuminated the first of the bomb cities, turning it into an inferno that erased 80 percent of its surface. The light burned, disintegrated or pulverized between 70 and 200 thousand of its inhabitants. Survivors faced an epidemic of leukemia, cancer and birth defects.

As if that were not enough, a second blinding light raised the temperature to 4,000 degrees celcius in the second bomb city, burning, desintegrating or pulverizing about 40,000 of its inhabitants.

Meanwhile, the top government officials of the country that caused the blinding light toasted in celebration of the project's success. All's fair in love and war (it's just a matter of sticking to the official definition —as the white-haired president taught us). The president of the country that led the attack did so against the wishes of scientists, parliamentarians, and even the general public.

The blinding light was, militarily speaking, a deliberate attack directed indiscriminately against the civilian population. There was no selection of military objectives.

The attack was engraved in the hearts of its authors as an act of heroism and a patriotic alliance between weapons and science.

The president of the country that threw the switch on the bomb cities informed the populace that it was done to shorten the agony and put an end to a long war.

In the end, there is still a lot of debate over whether the attack was strategically correct. Did it really reduce the losses from the war and accelerate the end, or was it overt genocide? The truth is that the bomb cities were an isolated event. There are those who estimate that conventional bombing had devastated 90 percent of the civilian population in seventy cities of the target country. So of course, there was no trial or public questioning of the victors.

The president who ordered the attack, a Mason, is highly admired within his own country. His image as a determined man has overshadowed the corruption scandals during his administration. Naturally, as the winner of the war, he never had to defend his decision to attack the bomb cities in a court of law. He did, however, get to watch as officials from other countries sat on the bench, accused of crimes against humanity.

Namely, if you're going go mad and start killing indiscriminately, you'd better win the war.

In other words:

All of these anecdotes, taken from real situations, represent just a few examples of genuine ethical and legal dilemmas. Certainly, other such examples sufficient to fill an entire book could be cited.

It would seem that only "poor people and idiots go to jail," as Mexican politician Álvaro Obregón has observed.

The truth is that white-collar crime is much more costly to society than run-of-the-mill street crime. Usually, white-collar crime goes unnoticed, as we have seen. And that is exactly what it's about: people with enough power and connections to elude justice. White-collar crime imitates the slippery skin of the Caribbean fish known as guavina. In other words, the success of a white-collar crime depends on how guavina-like the criminal is. To be able to achieve this, white-collar criminals have learned to master complex schemes, hire the best experts to navigate the twisting gaps between current laws, and project themselves through acts of charity (showing their best face to society). Social studies have shown that members of the elite often break the law, but as they have common interests, such faults go unnoticed. There are even studies indicating the existence of criminal networks within power groups, shamelessly woven for all manner of dark and selfish motives. There are authors who point to security and intelligence agencies as being conditioned to turn a blind eye to white collar crimes.

Practically speaking, there are times when it is very difficult to distinguish between organized crime, politicians and businessmen. By this, I do not mean that all politicians or all businessmen are criminals, but simply that the web of corruption links actors in different areas of the power elite. Sometimes, they are bound together so tightly within the web that they become inseparable, making it difficult to recognize who is who within the fabric.

On occasion, I have also wondered about the role of lawyers in social inequities. What responsibility do legal professionals have with regard to social justice?

In fact, corruption produces an asymmetry that deepens the competitive disadvantage of the most vulnerable groups within a society. Such asymmetry facilitates the increase in the number and magnitude of acts of corruption, leading to a vicious cycle of corruption and social inequity, as seen in many parts of the world.

All of this starts from the moment a naive society

relies on the goodwill of its leaders and their adherence to the norms established for "everyone equally."

There are times when, in order to understand the motives of a revolution, all that is needed is a little exploration of the level of public awareness regarding reality, whether past, present, or future.

Fortunately, we are not talking about criminals abusing the common good, but "great lords and honorable people."

Chapter 5:
The Inflamed Masses

"It is better to die standing, than to live on your knees."

— Emiliano Zapata

From the previous chapter, we are left with the question of why some situations engender enraged torch-bearing mobs or young people hurling Molotov cocktails, while other cases of great injustice are met with a paralysis reminiscent of a rookie rival thrown in the ring with Floyd Mayweather. What makes people react or hold on to their cell phone, protesting only on social media? What stirs the masses to answer the call to join in a revolt? Why is that sometimes no one shows up to protest, yet at other times people are able to overcome their fear of jail, torture, death, the boogeyman, the Terminator or even Chuck Norris?

History tells us that an inflamed mob can be a great organizer for the cause of justice, but it is also capable of committing horrible acts such as the crucifixion of Jesus of Nazareth or the Salem witch hunts. The crazed masses have also proven to be the main protagonists of the largest financial collapses throughout the centuries. All of this has its reasons. In the following pages we will seek to better understand the dynamics of protests as a common phase in the evolution of political revolutions.

The mob, its motives and its behavior

Psychologist and recipient of the Nobel Prize for economics Daniel Kahneman states in his book *Thinking Fast and Slow* that certain variables are taken into account when making decisions. These variables can be grouped into:

- Whether they imply winning or losing
- The probability of the gain or loss being realized
- The utility perceived by the individual

Our aversion to losing is consistently greater than our desire to win. This makes risk-taking desirable as long as it implies the chance of not losing. The likelihood of a gain or loss actually materializing enables us to find a point of balance between the probability, the amount to be won or lost, and the perceived utility. The perceived utility depends on the amount to be won or lost in relation to the assets of the individual (that is, for a millionaire, a small amount does not generate the same emotions as it would for a poor child). The emotions triggered by a loss are only balanced by a gain when the gain corresponds to approximately double the loss. The notion of utility increases or decreases with the amount earned or lost, but reaches a point where it no longer generates any significant emotional change.

When making a decision, therefore, it is done from an emotional state guided by the following equation:

[(Loss x 2) - (gain)] x [probability] x [notion of utility]

The aversion to losing can be correlated to the historical record of revolts arising from an increase in taxes or inflation (which produces a contraction in the purchasing power of individuals). A possible gain can also mobilize the masses, but it would have to be a much greater amount than the loss necessary to motivate the same masses. That is why it is easier to go out and protest to keep from losing a right than to recover a right already lost. Likewise, it is much more common for the government of country X to adopt an unpopular financial measure than one that would represent a substantial gain for the masses.

Additionally, it is known that it is usually more costly to win something you do not have, than to defend what you already have. This makes it easier to build a revolution around a threat of loss than around the challenge to the status quo.

Numerous studies have provided statistics indicating that riots occur in greater numbers and with greater violence in poorer geographical locations. Similarly, there are studies that correlate social violence with poverty. The possible reasons for this are multiple. First, the perception of loss is greater the less you have. Secondly, for someone who feels excluded, a protest not only implies the possibility of not losing but also of being taken into account, even if only as part of a group. Finally, a group of individuals who feel excluded from political decisions are more sensitive to certain measures taken by the police, which may make them feel even more excluded. The upper classes within a system (the successful types) do not usually feel excluded, since their proximity to (or participation in) the elite gives them access to political connections, media, marketing, etc. Even their Tweets and WhatsApp posts get more attention. So for the upper classes to participate in a revolt, there has to be serious instability or an extensive alteration of the current order.

The social validation that the multitude gives to a grievance instills a sense of the probability of success among its members. The more the excitement spreads, the greater becomes the perception of the probability of success. As a result, more individuals who were previously on the fence will make the decision to join the protest. In this way, a virtuous circle forms between the probability of success and the motivation-empowerment to join the crowd.

The movement of the masses can be predicted. Physicists have shown that the individual members respond to the same laws of physics that govern the behavior of particles. When a physical mass (many people in the same place at the same time) perceives itself as part of a group with a shared identity, it becomes a psychological mass. The psychological mass displays certain characteristics, such as walking more slowly and with greater coordination for longer distances. It is also comprised of larger subgroups, with closer physical proximity among the members. In a 2018 publication, Templeton, Drury and Philippides found that collective movement has been related to nonverbal communication, such as the speed and direction of movement of individuals. It has also been observed that those who pass near a psychological mass move faster and try to avoid it, keeping a greater distance than when the mass is only physical.

Just how does a psychologically united mass form? What causes its members to stop acting individually and adopt group behavior?

The transfer of thoughts from one mind to another has been demonstrated through various experiments in the last century, although some of these experiments have used questionable methodologies.

There are scientists such as Alejandro Perez who argue that interbrain electroencephalographic synchronization occurs during the activity of speaking and listening as a process that goes beyond simple verbal communication.[4] In another study using functional magnetic resonance imaging, it was found that following successful completion of a telepathic exercise, there was activation of the right parahippocampal gyrus (associated with spatial memory).[5]

4   Pérez, Alejandro, Manuel Carreiras, and Jon Andoni Duñabeitia. "Brain-to-Brain Entrainment: EEG Interbrain Synchronization While Speaking and Listening." *Scientific Reports* 7, no. 1 (2017). https://doi.org/10.1038/s41598-017-04464-4.

5   Venkatasubramanian, Ganesan, Peruvumban Jayakumar, Hongasandrar Nagendra, Dindagur Nagaraja, R Deeptha, and Bangaloren Gangadhar. "Investigating Para-

On the other hand, Guillaume Dumas argues that such synchronization occurs through social interaction, even when it is non-verbal. During the synchronization process, individuals begin to mimic each other and their brain activity begins to become similar, which can be recorded by electroencephalogram[6] (6).

To better understand this concept of interbrain synchronization, let's say that the neurons in our brain oscillate electrically in a rhythmic, synchronized manner. In the electrical brain activity recorded during an electroencephalogram, basically five bands are described. Waves are recorded at different frequencies for each band, which are named after the Greek letters gamma, beta, alpha, theta, and delta. Thus, gamma electrical activity allows us to learn and process information, beta gives us consciousness and allows us to solve problems, alpha allows us to relax, theta gives us creativity and intuition, and delta allows for biological repair during deep sleep.

Interbrain synchronization has been found to be related to the synchronization network in the alpha-mu bands of brain activity. How this occurs is not fully understood, however.[6]

normal Phenomena: Functional Brain Imaging of Telepathy." *International Journal of Yoga* 1, no. 2 (2008): 66. https://doi.org/10.4103/0973-6131.43543.

6   Dumas, Guillaume, Jacqueline Nadel, Robert Soussignan, Jacques Martinerie, and Line Garnero. "Inter-Brain Synchronization during Social Interaction." *PLoS ONE* 5, no. 8 (2010). https://doi.org/10.1371/journal.pone.0012166.

Interbrain synchronization presents us with multiple questions, such as the nature of the neurochemical or neuroelectric mechanisms that make it possible.

Interbrain synchronization also uses neural mechanisms of emotional perception. For example, Zhu, Lotte and colleagues described in 2018 that the greatest influence between individuals is produced by negative facial expressions.

Gestures in nonverbal communication are understood as part of the brain's mirroring system, which is simply the relationship between the observation of an action and the mental simulation of its execution (that is, if you see someone eating, you unconsciously imagine yourself eating too). This system, together with verbal communication, leads to intersubjectivity. In this way, previous attitudes and behaviors serve as a blueprint for subsequent social interactions and actions. We observe this effect in children's learning about posture and manners (for example), but we also see it in collective behaviors such as destruction of private property or vandalism. Furthermore, intersubjectivity refers to the implicit understanding of another person's emotions, as part of the common environment.

Interbrain communication relies on hormones such as oxytocin and vasopressin, as well as multiple neuronal mechanisms.[7] Yan Mu found that during coordination between individuals, there is synchronization in the neural oscillations of the alpha band. He also observed

---

7   Hari, Riitta, and Miiamaaria V. Kujala. "Brain Basis of Human Social Interaction: From Concepts to Brain Imaging." *Physiological Reviews* 89, no. 2 (2009): 453–79. https://doi.org/10.1152/physrev.00041.2007.

that the record of alpha band synchronization can predict better behavioral coordination between people. Similarly, he found that the hormone oxytocin shortened the time and increased the degree of synchronization.[8]

Interbrain synchronization has not only been studied in cooperative interactions. Both in situations of empathy and competition between individuals, involvement of the same area of the brain (the right posterior superior temporal sulcus) has been observed. The difference is marked by the intention and the attention given in the environmental context. Empathy not only promotes interbrain neural synchronization but has also been found to affect individual performance and the sense of cooperation, in the case of competitors.[9]

Everything mentioned so far implies some degree of connection through the senses (speech/hearing, visual, etc.), but there appears to be more to it than that. In terms of synchronization, there are still many mysteries to be uncovered beyond the role of the traditionally described senses.

It has been suggested that emotional states correspond to biomagnetic-metabolic fields which

---

8   Mu, Yan, Chunyan Guo, and Shihui Han. "Oxytocin Enhances Inter-Brain Synchrony during Social Coordination in Male Adults." *Social Cognitive and Affective Neuroscience* 11, no. 12 (2016): 1882–93. https://doi.org/10.1093/scan/nsw106.

9   Liu, Tao, Godai Saito, Chenhui Lin, and Hirofumi Saito. "Inter-Brain Network Underlying Turn-Based Cooperation and Competition: A Hyperscanning Study Using near-Infrared Spectroscopy." *Scientific Reports* 7, no. 1 (2017). https://doi.org/10.1038/s41598-017-09226-w.

may have structures for detection and transmission that facilitate their transfer between individuals with the increase of emotion within the crowd. It has been proposed that the mechanism may be similar to how transcranial magnetic stimulation acts on the limbic system. That is, there would be transmission of data from one brain to another through the oscillation of neural signals. Collective attention on the same focal point seems to lead to a mental state that allows for detection of threats in the environment and affects subsequent decision-making. We know that human psychology is susceptible to electromagnetic fields, and that the neuronal function of an individual can generate weak electromagnetic fields that alter the electromagnetic field of the individuals around him. The more individuals experiencing an emotion, the greater the alteration of the electromagnetic field, which could in turn affect even more individuals in the surrounding area.[10]

Revolutions usually involve youth. This fact is so conspicuous that it forces us to ask: What makes young people more belligerent? Inexperience? Do they feel they have less to lose? Do they ignore the potential risk they run? The truth is that in most movements there seems to be a race for control of the human mind, but particularly the minds of young people.

------

10 Mcdonnell, Alan. "The Sixth Sense-Emotional Contagion; Review of Biophysical Mechanisms Influencing Information Transfer in Groups." *Journal of Behavioral and Brain Science* 04, no. 07 (2014): 342–74. https://doi.org/10.4236/jbbs.2014.47035.

Science still has a long to-do list to achieve a better understanding of human thought and the interaction between our brain and our thoughts.

In any case, it takes two to tango, as they say. If on one side there are troublemakers, agitators, leaders, emotionally charged crowds with synchronized behavior and grievances, there will be those who make decisions from positions of power—and law enforcement—on the other.

Be that as it may, there is a synchronization that leads the crowd to a collective anger, in turn provoking one of two political responses: criminalize what has happened or try to understand the reasons for the revolt, together with all of the possible consequences. In any event, it is a group mentality that comes into play during riots, with an intuitive interaction between the players (described above). This pattern of interaction has been studied by psychologists, resulting in two scientific models to address the phenomenon. One of the models follows patterns, while the other is based on the transmission of emotions. The pattern approach serves to predict the behavior of the multitude in the face of an unexpected event in order to allow for disaster planning and prevention. The behaviors displayed in street protests, however, can be unpredictable due to the multiple variables involved. For this reason it is preferable to use the emotion transmission model to better understand them. In this model, there is unconscious emotional contagion among the participants, which can grow into a social contagion. During social contagion there is a flood of information being passed along that encourages decision-making based on the social approval of previous decisions made by others, even if these decisions break the law and threaten public order. The emotions that are transmitted are mainly panic and collective hysteria. Both can lead to vandalism or trigger a spiral of violence, especially when police handling of the situation management reinforces the feeling of social exclusion.[11]

There are times when individuals feel that forming a mob is the only weapon of political resistance available against the threat of change, change that is often imposed by the elite with the idea that it is good, brings progress, and is driven by people with some kind of superiority over the uncultured or illiterate masses. The idea of anonymity within the crowd, as well as the notion of dilution of responsibility among group members, makes it easier for individual acts of violence to occur. These behaviors can spread within the group as individuality is replaced by an unconscious or group mentality, causing individual behaviors to coalesce into group behavior. Usually, the police and other members of law enforcement are the first to be targeted by violence. In the second stage, aggression is directed against private and public property (depending on the group's motives), with sporadic destruction, especially of symbolic sites. Once the mob has synchronized psychologically, it loses the ability to reason and moves unpredictably. Mismanagement of this concept by the police leads to the belief that the only way to control the situation is through the use of force, which only

11 Gross, Michael. "Why Do People Riot?" *Current Biology* 21, no. 18 (2011). https://doi.org/10.1016/j. cub.2011.09.015.

generates more violence. The mob identifies its cause as legitimate, so the use of force by the police only causes their own authority to lose legitimacy. The use of force can also lead to the radicalization of the more moderate members of the mob.[12]

Law enforcement

Law enforcement, then, has two options for maintaining control of the situation: to suppress and/or to negotiate. Suppression as such has been falling into disuse (as a first option), because it is known that use of this tactic from the onset will only lead to more violent clashes, resulting in greater numbers of injured and greater material damage. Whether for purposes of suppression or negotiation, the gathering of intelligence, including the identification of leaders and circulating information, is necessary. The identification of inaccurate or false information that is being circulated can be addressed in traditional media and social networks as a form of prevention. The battle of circulating information usually ends in a competition to conquer public opinion and the emotions of the majority. Current technology allows disturbances to be recorded with sufficient resolution to identify those who break the law or cause harm to other individuals or to public or private property. In addition to identification for police purposes, the circulation of videos or photos in social networks and media helps to

---

12   Stott, Clifford, and John Drury. "Contemporary Understanding of Riots: Classical Crowd Psychology, Ideology and the Social Identity Approach." *Public Understanding of Science* 26, no. 1 (2016): 2–14. https://doi.org/10.1177/0963662516639872.

generate social and moral sanction of the individuals engaged in these destructive behaviors.

Public surveillance cameras, as well as the widespread use of cell phones, have made anonymity increasingly difficult, which may explain why in the last decade young people have been less likely to protest publicly.

Currently, active management by the police begins with intimidation of the mob (including their physical presence, assuming a combat formation, the appearance of their uniforms, equipment, etc.) as a way of discouraging the protest. This intimidation causes the protesters to perceive a decreased likelihood of winning, and increases the possible net loss that might be incurred due to arrest or physical injury.

Crowd control police are instructed to maintain control of their emotions (so that a cascade of emotions similar to that of the crowd does not arise), taking into account that excessive aggression can generate more violence (like the situation that led to the Boston massacre).

For the police, it is important to distinguish between a protest that violates the law and a peaceful demonstration in compliance with the law.

If the mob is connected psychologically, the police are at a numerical disadvantage to control it, so in addition to a psychological connection they must also be tactically connected as a team (Remember the Bolsheviks: the most organized team always wins). The tactical connection is provided by the protocols for the different stages (including the use of force) and the planning of the approach, in order to respond to any of the possible avenues that a protest can take.

The best tool to defuse mass fury is dialogue in which both civil authorities and police participate. In fact, there are multiple accounts of governments that have already adopted the tactic of initiating a fictitious dialogue in order to stall for time while applying an unpopular measure.

Amiability and dialogue with the crowd can be a way to reduce stress, since it makes them feel they are being paid attention (not excluded). Even a smile can spread and compete with the anger that drove the crowd to gather in the first place. The police should always keep in mind that their goal is to maintain order and protect the safety of individuals and of public and private property. Security forces should never see protesters as "enemies." The ideal goal is to calm the crowd and get individuals to disperse and go home. Confrontation is a last resort which should be avoided at all costs.

It has been found that the presence of firearms in the front lines of the crowd control police is interpreted as a invitation to escalate the violence. It even tempts protesters to try to capture the weapons, which they could then use to fire back at the police.

The police are usually better armed than the troublemakers, but tactics to prevent bodily harm have been improving in recent decades. Among these tactics is the identification and arrest of leaders who act as agitators or incite the crowd to increased levels of violence. Gaps in the police formation give the less violent the opportunity to escape and go home.

Recap

Simply put, a revolt can be summarized in the following steps:

1. People find out about the problem and information begins to circulate, speculations are made and biases emerge, usually involving the perception of "loss" by certain individuals (mainly the most vulnerable)
2. The situation is analyzed on an individual basis and an equation begins to take shape in people's minds which will vary according to the possible gain/loss, probability and notion of (individual) utility. This equation will be dynamic and will continue to be nourished by the information that is generated over time
3. Individuals begin to take stock of the environment around them, in search of social approval to act by referring to the behavior of others in the same environment (which can modify the probability variable within the individual mental equation
4. A decision is made on whether or not to answer the call
5. If the call is answered, the individual once again takes stock of the environment. Their mental equation remains active and dynamic
6. Meanwhile, the process of interbrain synchronization is causing collective behavior to take control of the individual mind that was keeping track of its equation

7. The next step is taken by law enforcement, which will divide its actions between two options: negotiate and suppress

8. A dynamic reconsideration is made by the individual, who must decide whether to remain in the group or turn control back over to the individual mind and its equation, which serves to protect the survival instinct

Chapter 6:
The Leader

"My job is not to be easy on people..."
— Steve Jobs

Today, leadership seems to be a sublime quality derived from the wisdom emanating from somewhere between the Great Beyond and the latest scheme invented by the cleverest of modern administration gurus. There are innumerable leadership theories, all trying to explain or predict the possibility of a group's success, of making a better salary in a managerial position, or of having greater influence as a political leader.

According to some, leadership is intrinsic to us and is in our DNA, similar to how dominance and social hierarchy work in animals. There are studies that support the idea that leadership is intrinsic to our nature, with genetics representing about 30 percent of leadership qualities.[13]

---

13 Hadhazy, Adam. "Life's Extremes: Leaders vs. Followers." LiveScience. Purch, November 20, 2011. https://www.livescience.com/17116-life-extremes-leaders-followers.html.

Personally, I prefer to continue thinking that leadership is intrinsic to every human being in certain areas, circumstances and moments in life.

While we may think there are areas in which different individuals stand out more, as well as circumstances that enhance leadership abilities, there is no universal formula nor a mold that can be applied to everyone. In fact, the skill depends on both the circumstances and the characteristics of the person. Both can make you an excellent leader in one group, and a total fiasco in another.

Returning to the subject of revolutions, it can be said that within the social fabric, leadership is woven with three strands: power, status, and legitimacy.

According to Kevin Kruse, leadership is the process of social influence in which the efforts of others are maximized towards achieving a goal. Kruse says it has nothing to do with age, academic degrees, personal attributes (such as dominance or charisma) or hierarchy, but it does have key elements such as social influence and the definition of at least one objective.[14]

The leader of a multitude doesn't have to be the founder and doesn't even have to remain part of it. They are simply a figure that maintains stability within the group. In popular culture, it is understood that a good leader must cultivate discipline within the team, as well as provide the team with training in tactics to achieve its goals.

---

14 Kruse, Kevin. "What Is Leadership?" Forbes. Forbes Magazine, September 2, 2015. https://www.forbes.com/sites/kevinkruse/2013/04/09/what-is-leadership/?sh=c-9b5e245b90c.

Of course, in a multitude, only a limited percentage will be willing to make a serious commitment in a given moment. Of that limited number, only a few will be willing to assume the responsibilities that leadership implies. This distribution could be understood as: 20 percent will commit for the 80 percent (that does not commit), and only 20 percent of the committed 20 percent will assume leadership (if we apply the Pareto principle, or 80/20 rule, which states that 20 percent of the input produces 80 percent of the results). In other words, four-out-of-100.

It is not surprising that there are those who want to lead the group, since we human beings tend to construct an optimistic image of ourselves that makes us feel we are special or stand out from the crowd in some area. This optimistic and distorted view causes us to overestimate our abilities, achievements, etc. Of course, mathematically, most of us fall well within the normal distribution curve, but for some reason we all like to believe that we are better than the rest.

But don't lose heart, dear reader. Regardless of where we find ourselves in the distribution curve, we all have the ability to exert some degree of influence within society. According to sociologists, an introvert influences 10,000 people during an average lifetime.[15]

Recent advances in the neurosciences have allowed us to better understand how the human brain works, including in matters of leadership. Efforts have been

---

15 Elmore, Tim. "Is Everyone a Leader?" Psychology Today. Sussex Publishers, February 20, 2014. https://www.psychologytoday.com/us/blog/artificial-maturity/201402/is-everyone-leader.

made to understand the functioning of the brain of both leaders and followers, which has led to the appearance of numerous conjecturers and purveyors of services that promise fast and effective learning of the ABC's of leadership (part of the race to be the cleverest guru, as mentioned before).

Research on brain functioning traditionally states that leadership implies a sort of kidnapping of the amygdala of followers. The amygdala is a part of our brain with functions related to memory, decision-making, and basic emotional responses such as fear and anger. Now, there is a science to kidnapping the amygdala, meaning that whoever takes the role of leader in directing a group towards an objective must have the ability to stir the emotions of the members of that group. Since the human mind has evolved to ensure survival, changes are often seen as threats (generating fear), so leaders must focus on the positive aspects of the necessary changes.

It is true that regardless of how much neuro-whatever we study, we are still far from understanding the human brain. Aspects such as the oscillatory phenomenon in the exchange of data among members of a crowd have also been implicated in the mechanics of leadership. According to this theory, there are people who emit signals that exert greater influence over others, meaning that a leader's ability lies in getting others to emit similar brain waves. Alan McDonnell, in 2014, proposed a possible biophysical mechanism in order to understand this function. In his hypothesis, he states that the ability to lead is expressed as data patterns, where the leader's biomagnetic signal is spread among the followers, so that the patterns of the followers become similar to those of the leader. and vice versa.

In a nutshell, what is known about the human brain as it applies to leadership is that the leader makes reason stand aside and causes emotions to begin to vibrate at a single frequency, in unison, in the members of the influenced group.

Leadership or transfer*ence*?

According to psychoanalyst and anthropologist Michael Macoby, leaders are usually the heroes who motivate us to reach places we would not reach without them. Leaders usually have two characteristics: exceptional talent, and the ability to attract followers. The problems start when the identity of the followers is ignored and they are overshadowed by the charisma of the leader. This can make it harder to secure followers. Those who follow, do so for both rational and irrational reasons (such as the need for protection or authority that a father gives, or the need for consensus that a brother can give).

Macoby argues that the transference of previous experiences, as described by Sigmund Freud, is the key to understanding leadership theories and the behavior of human organizations. Not all transferences are positive and their nature can change over time, but in general, they seem to be the glue that binds followers to a leader, whom they see as more intelligent, more pleasant, or more charismatic than he (or she) really is. The leader in turn projects his experiences on his followers, which is called countertransference. Transference is both a source of strength for leaders as well as a threat, since it introduces subjectivity into the relationship. The expectations to which followers hold their leader can also vary according to the culture and the society.

Without a doubt, some of the best leaders become adept at manipulating the paternal transference of their followers. Maternal transference implies authority, but also empathy and affection from the leader, who does not necessarily have to be a woman. Sibling transference can be ambivalent and make it difficult to exercise authority, but has become more common as the concept of authority has changed in Western culture.[16]

The truth is that leadership emerges circumstantially, meaning that there are no two identical situations and no two identical results for the same leader. As with animals, leadership traits are not exclusive to temperament and personality; leadership also depends on size and certain physical traits, which exercise much greater influence than previously thought.

Next, we will look at some features associated with leadership.

The face of leadership

While we like to think that leadership is a product of hard work, ability, special skills, knowledge, or even charisma, certain key physical characteristics have been

---

16   Maccoby, Michael. "Why People Follow the Leader: The Power of Transference." Harvard Business Review, August 1, 2014. https://hbr.org/2004/09/why-people-follow-the-leader-the-power-of-transference.

identified. Without a doubt, when it comes to choosing leaders, men have the advantage over women. Height is another factor, given that 30 percent of senior leaders in the United States stand over six-feet-two-inches tall (representing only 4 percent of Americans). Similarly, men in high-ranking positions tend to have deeper voices. It has also been observed that when bosses exercise and are in good physical condition, the organizations they lead tend to perform better.[17]

But the correlation doesn't stop at physical height; the accompanying facial features are linked to success both in political leadership and in the corporate world.

There are facial features that are associated with dominance, such as a square face, pronounced jawline, prominent eyebrows, and small eyes. These characteristics are good in certain circumstances, but can be negative in others. It has been found that these same traits also generate distrust, and in certain circumstances, inspiring trust can be more valuable than establishing dominance.[18]

Facial characteristics are so relevant to the circumstances that there are reports that features such as a large mouth and broad face are associated with greater leadership in a company, while the opposite facial

17 Baer, Drake. "3 Physical Qualities People Associate With Great Leaders—For Better Or Worse." Business Insider, October 8, 2014. https://www.businessinsider.in/3-physical-qualities-people-associate-with-great-leaders-for-better-or-worse/articleshow/44723210.cms.

18 "The Look of Leadership." Association for Psychological Science - APS, December 15, 2015. https://www.psychologicalscience.org/blog/the-look-of-leadership.html.

characteristics are associated with greater leadership in non-profit organizations.[19]

Additionally, there are studies that have found that facial symmetry and attractiveness predispose a person to success in life and business. That is to say, there is a subclass of ugly people (of which I may be part) who are victims of a type of discrimination that is traditionally overlooked. Likewise, it is said that faces that reflect greater maturity also provide an advantage in terms of the probability of assuming leadership.[20]

From the time we are children, we associate the beauty of a face with intelligence. In the same way, we relate the symmetry of a face to honesty, even though no real relationship exists between such variables.[21] In fact, there are reports that no anthropometric characteristic has demonstrated any relationship to the performance of an individual in a leadership position.[22]

19   McGregor, Jena. "How a CEO's Face Could Predict His Success." The Washington Post. WP Company, April 7, 2019. https://www.washingtonpost.com/news/on-leadership/wp/2016/07/05/how-a-ceos-face-could-predict-his-success/.

20   Cherulnik, Paul D., Laurie C. Turns, and Scott K. Wilderman. "Physical Appearance and Leadership: Exploring The Role of Appearance-Based Attribution in Leader Emergence." *Journal of Applied Social Psychology* 20, no. 18 (1990): 1530–39. https://doi.org/10.1111/j.1559-1816.1990.tb01491.x.

21   Ludden, David. "The Look of a Leader." Psychology Today. Sussex Publishers, August 26, 2017. https://www.psychologytoday.com/us/blog/talking-apes/201708/the-look-leader.

22   Stoker, Janka I., Harry Garretsen, and Luuk J. Spreeuwers. "The Facial Appearance of CEOs: Faces Signal

Nevertheless, examples of absurd relationships abound, such as the fact that for women, just being blonde can represent a 7 percent increase in earnings over brunettes. A fit body generates a similar effect.[23]

All of this leads to the idea that an equation could be made to determine the level of leadership of an individual at a given moment. Of course, we have variables such as temperament, dominance, physical height, voice, physical condition, mouth size, eye size, facial symmetry, facial attractiveness, hair color, etc., but these variables are highly subjective. It would be so difficult to establish how much each variable contributes, particularly since the weight of that contribution varies depending on the circumstance, that coming up with an equation of some scientific value is nearly impossible. Despite all this, I would not be surprised if at some point some clairvoyant, futuristic administration guru or neuro-whatever appears, to bestow on us his esoteric recipe in a formula that applies to everyone.

The truth is that the concept of physical characteristics being predictive of the ability of a leader only introduces biases when selecting who will lead the next revolution. In other words, it is a form of discrimination that traditionally we were not aware of. There seems to be a psychosocial tendency to attribute

Selection but Not Performance." *Plos One* 11, no. 7 (2016). https://doi.org/10.1371/journal.pone.0159950.

23   Harsh, Anurag. "Does Attractiveness and Appearance Equate to Leadership and Career Success?" HuffPost. HuffPost, September 15, 2017. https://www.huffpost.com/entry/does-attractiveness-and-appearance-equate-to-leadership_b_59ba734be4b02c642e4a1414.

negative traits to those who are less physically endowed. To give an example, it would have been much more difficult for an ugly, poor, sick old woman to escape the bonfire if accused of witchcraft in the Middle Ages, even more so if she suffered from mental illness.

This does not mean that individuals lacking the physical characteristics of the leadership stereotype cannot ascend; it will simply take more work, and they will have to exaggerate the characteristics within their reach, such as dominance, aggressiveness, and perhaps even their level of knowledge.

The dark side

Once the leader has taken his place within the social fabric, history begins to change.

It is not uncommon to see ordinary people (like the vast majority of us) become participants, accomplices or authors, both material and intellectual, of all kinds of evil after reaching a position of power.

Leaders, like every human being, can discover the dark side of their personality when they assume a social role they have not occupied before. The eminent social psychologist Phil Zimbardo, who has made a career studying the psychology of evil, states that under the right social conditions, most people abandon their moral principles and are capable of committing acts that would normally be unthinkable for them. Frequently, inhuman acts are carried out under the pretext that they will lead to a "superior good," not with the idea that an act of evil is being committed. Zimbardo's approach is important because it allows us to understand this type of behavior.

According to Bill George, the powerful can lose their way and even their moral principles, which suggests that future leaders must be prepared to confront enormous complexities and pressures. The public often points to political leaders as bad or evil. Leaders who become derailed in their social trajectory are not necessarily bad people, but have simply succumbed to the temptations in their way. There are leaders who impose their will regardless of the people they destroy along the way, which can leave them feeling paranoid and insecure about the loyalty of others. This can cause their organization to lose touch with reality and be exposed to multiple dangers, which they usually blame on others. Despite all these possible transformations, it can be said that aspiring to positions of power does not necessarily have to be bad. Positions of power can be used to serve a large group or society as a whole.[24]

On the other hand, there are teachings such as those imparted by former United States secretary of defense Robert McNamara in the documentary *Fog of War*, in which he says, "to do good, you may have to engage in evil." McNamara refers to the fact that even if the ultimate goal is noble, there are times when leaders may come up with plans that set aside good practices or appropriate ethical behavior. The big question comes later: "How much evil can we do, to do good?"

The ideological platform often becomes the perfect justification to lead the group towards a

---

24 George, Bill. "Why Leaders Lose Their Way." HBS Working Knowledge, June 6, 2011. https://hbswk.hbs.edu/item/why-leaders-lose-their-way.

seemingly essential goal to which allegiance "must" be sworn. Obedience is reinforced when there are rigid rules to adhere to. That way, those who obey can feel that even though they are doing something uncomfortable, they are contributing to a sublime and transcendental cause. In addition, the person who complies usually perceives that the responsibility lies with the person giving the order.

Along with ideology there can also be hate speech, which can be a magnet for radicals but creates a barrier to any mature discussion about problems. Ideologies accompanied by hate speech can leave scars that linger for generations. The most curious thing is that hate speech does not necessarily have to look like "hate speech." Hate speech may seem more like a firm stance taken by a potential leader who is sure of himself and sure that he has the truth and that his approach is the right one. Such a position can be the product of a biased logic that ends up rationalizing and justifying a conceptual error. The "firm stance" discourse may include rhetoric that directs a "challenge" (not exactly hate) at those who oppose their thinking. For a fanatic or radical, this can be an incredibly attractive position to follow and support. In practical terms, such a seemingly good and firm position ends up provoking social polarization and generating hatred between two divergent views. Positions of hate, which are merely a demonstration of verticality in the morality, beliefs, or convictions of those who support them, can end up generating verbal, psychological, and even physical violence, especially if the hatred is directed at a minority or other vulnerable group within society. The result is a social dichotomization that transforms virtually every single person into a friend or enemy, all due to the lack of capacity for complex analysis and adequate knowledge to gauge reality.

A rhetoric of hate worth studying for all its ramifications is that of Nazi Germany. According to Tyler Cowen, the Germans followed Hitler because he made them feel important as well as protected by a warm-hearted State, through social benefits that endure to this day. Radical positions were presented as merely part of a good cause. The truth is that those positions led to horrors that I will not enter into on this occasion.[25] Unfortunately, the Nazi atrocities were only the materialization of Hitler's twisted thinking as expressed in his book *Mein Kampf*, where he asserted that ideological revolutions had to be imposed by force, if necessary.

Apart from radicalization, strong leaders present other risks, not only for other social actors but also for the organizations they lead. Strong leadership that coincides with a cohesive group can lead to groupthink, a phenomenon that was thoroughly investigated by psychologist Irving Janis in the 1970s. In groupthink, a group of individuals conforms to a biased understanding

---

25   Tyler Cowen March 30, 2005 at 7:47 am in Political Science. "Why Did so Many Germans Support Hitler?" Marginal REVOLUTION, March 30, 2005. https://marginalrevolution.com/marginalrevolution/2005/03/why_did_so_many.html.

of reality that leads to bad decisions. In other words, errors of perception in the feedback received by the group can cause it to make bad decisions repeatedly, without any awareness of it. Such skewed and erroneous feedback within a group is a good excuse to moonwalk to the nearest exit, in the best Michael Jackson style.

Once you've got a good cohesive group equipped with a specific ideology, hate-filled ideas (that everyone thinks are just firm convictions), a strong leader and an appropriately slanted perception of reality, the only ingredient missing is the cherry on top. At this point, another bias may appear: the gap between "them" and "us" that causes a society to divide. Both sides begin to regard the other as a subclass, as "despicable," or simply as less than human.

According to social psychologist Philip Zimbardo in his book *The Lucifer Effect*, cruelty, like any wrongdoing, is nothing more than a social behavior (corresponding to a situation within a system) in which there is active complicity by some, the silent complicity of others, and the deactivation of the victims, especially when the latter suffer from learned hopelessness. Those who take the initiative and assume leadership to commit evil acts may be seeking recognition or promotion within a group (which reminds me of the comic strip of the dictator who was always talking about what bad thing he would like to have happen to a certain political adversary, and sure enough, some lackey would do the job just to ingratiate himself). The leader is crucial to evildoing, because authority-obedience is key to the dilution of responsibility that an individual needs to commit any kind of atrocity.

So, does all this mean that there are incredibly good leaders who stand leagues apart from the evil leaders that lose their way and succumb to temptation? I think the question is not worth answering. But I'll leave you with this thought: Mongolian leader Genghis Khan is traditionally portrayed as bloodthirsty and implacable, and has been credited with the death of 40 million people (approximately 10 percent of the global population at that time). So great was the scale of the killing, there are those who claim it caused a drop in atmospheric CO_2! Nevertheless, Genghis Khan is credited with the following axiom: "A leader can never be happy until his people are happy."

In crisis

While it is true that leaders can drag entire populations down the wrong path, it is also true that they sometimes ally with the authorities to handle crises for the collective benefit.

In crowd management, negotiation between the current authority and crowd leaders can avert many problems. It can prevent riots, injuries and destruction to public and private property. Even after riots erupt, negotiation with crowd leaders can help calm tempers or encourage people to abandon the protest and go home.

In a 2007 paper, Moshe Pinkert describes the challenges of crowd control, especially when there are casualties from clashes with the police. Citing the lessons learned from riots in Nazareth, he states that the role of leaders is key to controlling the masses in the hospital area, where first responders attend to the injured. He ends by recommending that leaders be familiar with the emergency care procedures practiced by health personnel.[26]

Whether acting for the common good or out of selfishness, the essence of leadership lies in exercising control of the human mind within a collective. And that is exactly what the next chapter is about.

---

26 Pinkert, Moshe, Yuval Bloch, Dagan Schwartz, Isaac Ashkenazi, Bishara Nakhleh, Barhoum Massad, Michal Peres, and Yaron Bar-Dayan. "Leadership as a Component of Crowd Control in a Hospital Dealing with a Mass-Casualty Incident: Lessons Learned from the October 2000 Riots in Nazareth." *Prehospital and Disaster Medicine* 22, no. 6 (2007): 522–26. https://doi.org/10.1017/s1049023x00005367.

Chapter 7:
Control of the human mind—
The most coveted jewel

"If you don't know jewelry, know the jeweler."

— Warren Buffet

As a species, we pride ourselves on being the pinnacle of complexity in the universe. We have explored outer space only to realize that we don't know enough about our own body or its crowning jewel, our brain, much less our most precious social jewel, the human mind.

The human mind is the product of a wonderful piece of machinery: our brain. Without entering into an exhausting debate about whether this is a materialistic neurological concept, we cannot deny that the activity of our neurons is paramount to the origin of our thoughts and emotions.

We have been trying for centuries to decipher how this machine and its complex nervous connections work, but continue to be frustrated in our quest to fully understand how human thinking is generated. We have resigned ourselves to using only a certain amount of knowledge in a somewhat amateurish fashion to try to manipulate people's minds for purposes of marketing, doing business, gaining political clout, etc.

We tend to overestimate our current technology. For example, we overestimate the power of social networks, just as we overestimated the Internet in the 1990s or just about any other invention that seemed novel at a given point in history.

Despite our continued ignorance, the professionalism that is being developed with respect to social manipulation is surprising. This quest for perfection promises rapid progress, thanks to new advances in the neurosciences and the interest of the markets in conquering the human mind.

In the search to control what has seemed uncontrollable, humanity has undertaken to study the human mind with the same audacity we employ to study geosolar engineering in order to conduct large-scale manipulation of the atmosphere and climate at our whim.[27]

The mind control that is being sought is nothing more or less than the alteration of an individual's behavior in an observable way, without the consent of the controlled individual, and for a specific purpose.[28]

---

27   Higgins, Abigail. "10 Ways the World Is Most Likely to End, Explained by Scientists." Vox. Vox, October 18, 2018. https://www.vox.com/future-perfect/2018/10/18/17957162/nuclear-war-asteroid-volcano-science-climate-change.

28   Koivuniemi, Andrew, and Kevin Otto. "When altering Brain Function Becomes mind Control." *Frontiers in*

We might ask whether such a thing as mind control is even possible. Well, the search to control the human mind has led to the development of sciences such as ethology, which is simply the scientific study of animal behavior in a mixture of field and laboratory studies.[29]

The objective of ethology is to identify the characteristics of the stimuli that trigger a particular reaction in different animals, or which reactions to expect for a given stimulus. In this way, ethology seeks to trigger certain behaviors without passing through the filter of consciousness.

Traditionally, we know that there are fundamental principles that direct human behavior, these being the reward, punishment and reinforcement of certain behaviors. However, interest in mind control coincides with the fact that we are living in what appears to be the era of neurosciences, an era driven precisely by research to better understand the functioning of the brain and mind, which will subsequently be the subject of control.

It is not surprising, then, that we begin to identify concepts such as neuroethology, which studies the neural mechanisms of animal behavior. Apparently, thinking problems and algorithms are widespread in nature, with similarities among different species. This would imply

Systems Neuroscience 8 (2014). https://doi.org/10.3389/fnsys.2014.00202.

29 "Ethology." Encyclopædia Britannica. Encyclopædia Britannica, Inc. Accessed November 16, 2020. https://www.britannica.com/science/ethology.

a fundamental structural design of the nervous system which has been perfected through evolution.[30]

Since humans are animals, this knowledge leads to the development of new mechanisms to induce the obedience of a multitude with fewer opportunities for analysis, reasoning and critical thinking.

We now come to the moment when the reader might begin to question the objectivity of my arguments, in the middle of a chapter that seems to come straight from the annals of conspiracy theories or the depths of popular superstition.

Well, let's look at the subject a little more closely. Professor Robert Cialdini, in his book *Influence: The Psychology of Persuasion*, suggests that we are surrounded by things we do not need, we do things that do not benefit us, we seek to have things that do not help us, and we even sympathize with politicians who harm and steal from us. All thanks to the influence of marketing. We are hypnotized by social networks, advertising and the media. Many times, freedom of thought is nothing more than an illusion in the midst of that hypnosis. The next time you feel tempted to buy something, ask yourself this: Why do I want it? Because I like it? You may find the answer disturbing. You will realize that we are continuously manipulated, day in and day out.

Cialdini also states that the accelerated pace of modern life deprives us of conditions for careful

---

30 Adams, Geoffrey K, Karli K Watson, John Pearson, and Michael L Platt. "Neuroethology of Decision-Making." *Current Opinion in Neurobiology* 22, no. 6 (2012): 982–89. https://doi.org/10.1016/j.conb.2012.07.009.

analysis. It is true that we are increasingly vulnerable to the use of tools that induce our obedience automatically. Quite simply, our lives and our activities have become increasingly complex, to the point of overwhelming our biological capacity. This causes us to stop reasoning about decisions and facts that seem minor, defaulting instead to an automated, intuitive mode. The main tools that induce our obedience are the sense of reciprocity, appealing to our commitment and consistency with what we say, our need for social approval, linking our obedience with something we like, subordinating our obedience to some kind of authority, and the perception of scarcity of something desirable.

Cialdini's arguments are not conspiratorial, they are part of the training of any seller or student of marketing or advertising. However, he overlooks marketing tactics that are considered unethical and are also widely used, such as deceptive advertising, manipulation of internet links to increase the mention of a brand, emotional exploitation, contacting potential clients without their consent, and even assuming a humanistic position to unleash a public controversy that increases the visibility of a brand.[31]

On fear

There are also negative influences used to induce moods or other types of obedience. Whether

_____

31 DeMers, Jayson. "5 Borderline Unethical Marketing Practices: Are You Guilty?" Medium. Medium, May 11, 2020. https://jaysondemers.medium.com/5-borderline-unethical-marketing-practices-are-you-guilty-d5c7ce745e01.

consciously or unconsciously (because bad news simply sells more), repeated exposure to disturbing images or videos through the media is associated with mental and physical disorders. We are constantly exposed to collective psychological traumas which can be lasting and alter the behavior of our societies.[32]

Unfortunately, most of the media are simply businesses, and as such, they exploit whatever catches the public's attention to improve their billing.

Repeated collective psychological trauma creates an environment of fear around various issues. Fear is nothing more than anxiety in anticipation of an event or an imagined experience. Many times such anxiety is capable of causing more damage than the imagined event itself.

Fear generates an individual reaction to a physical or even socio-political threat, and is an essential tool in the political control of those who feel particularly vulnerable. It is internalized or externalized in behaviors of fleeing or fighting, subjugation, or rebellion.[33]

Fear is so useful that it is one of the tools used par excellence to get people to give up their freedom.

It is not only fear that feeds social stress and anxiety: negative rhetoric has also been associated with

32 "Repeated Exposure to Traumatic Images May Be Harmful to Health." ScienceDaily. ScienceDaily, September 4, 2012. https://www.sciencedaily.com/releases/2012/09/120904150108.htm.

33 Barbalet, Jack, and Nicolas Demertzis. "Collective Fear and Societal Change." *Emotions in Politics*, 2013, 167–85. https://doi.org/10.1057/9781137025661_9.

stress, and with a lower perception of health and well-being by those who listen to it.[34]

We are left, then, asking ourselves the big question: If so many people are becoming so sophisticated and knowledgeable in social control...could it be that we live in a puppet society in which the masses do not control the information or criteria? Could it be that our society does not have the knowledge, the capacity, or the opportunity to make decisions in what is only a facade of democracy? Could it be that Western democracies, like the freedom of which we boast so much, are nothing more than an illusion?

A puppet society?

Like the other neurosciences, psychology is increasingly identified as a tool of social control, causing many experts in the field to assert that the discipline has lost its way. They argue that psychology is being used to perpetuate social injustices and has been usurped by marketing to become a political activity. The military sector has also invested heavily in research along these lines, leading to broad social consequences.[35] The discipline that has

34 Chavez, Leo R., Belinda Campos, Karina Corona, Daina Sanchez, and Catherine Belyeu Ruiz. "Words Hurt: Political Rhetoric, Emotions/Affect, and Psychological Well-Being among Mexican-Origin Youth." *Social Science & Medicine* 228 (2019): 240–51. https://doi.org/10.1016/j.socscimed.2019.03.008.

35 "Agents of Social Control?" Agents of social control? | The Psychologist. Accessed November 16, 2020. https://thepsychologist.bps.org.uk/volume-20/edition-7/agents-social-control.

made so many contributions to humanity seems to be changing in purpose. It has passed from caring for the individual to dominating or even oppressing individuals. However, like other scientific disciplines, psychology is subject to economic and political forces that reduce the space for debate on the ethical questions around its transformation.[36]

An example of how psychology is applied in social control can be seen when media and social networks join forces to villainize someone considered a threat by a power group. This villain image becomes implanted in the limbic system of the public, causing an array of emotions to be unleashed. At the same time, the "villain" is stripped of his human characteristics (he is dehumanized). The emotional implant, together with the perception of dehumanization by the public, triggers automatic reactions that can unfold without passing through the filter of reason. Thus, we see entire communities clamoring for the death of a human being who is the victim of a given circumstance and socio-historical moment, from Bible times to the French Revolution to the gallows of Saddam Hussein.

The dehumanization of the figure of the "villain" (to whom we were introduced in the previous chapter, and who in the right circumstances may have been a hero or a great lord), leads our brain to dichotomously understand the separation between "them" and "us." This dichotomous social perception together with

---

36 Shallice, T. "Psychology and Social Control." *Cognition* 17, no. 1 (1984): 29–48. https://doi.org/10.1016/0010-0277(84)90041-6.

the interpretation of "the enemy" causes individuals to perceive a threat, which generates fear, and all this is combined with the social prejudices existing at the moment.

Now, political control through psychological manipulation is not exactly the best practice, even for politicians who believe they benefit from it. Politicians are doing their countries a disservice when they choose to influence potential voters in this manner. Taking advantage of the lack of critical thinking to manipulate the public only makes society less collaborative. This lack of critical thinking also manifests as a lack of interest in understanding the problems or in analyzing possible solutions, much less in taking an active role to be part of the solution.

When René Descartes said "I think, therefore I am," he could have been suggesting that for groups that advocate for social control, the controlled masses are also dehumanized, just like the "villain" they seek to hang or decapitate.

A not-so-rational reasoning

It is easy to place all the blame for manipulation of the masses on the economic and political power of the elite, but now let's look at the other side of the coin. Everything can be coming up roses until the day a society is pierced by the devil's sharpest claw: speculation.

We speculate every time the beliefs of our superstitious minds latch on to an illusion. The illusion can be about something bad, like the End Times (foretold innumerable times throughout the last millennium, without the clock stopping to date), or about something good, as the major stock exchanges can attest.

Speculation is nothing more than a scantly thought out or reasoned theory about something. Speculation is what makes us anticipate that a certain number will play in the lottery, we will come up with a million-dollar business idea or a huge tragedy will occur. Speculation can be so strong that it is capable of inducing all the members of a sect to commit suicide under the belief that the world is going to end.

Illusion is a poor mental representation of a sensory stimulus, or simply an interpretation that contradicts objective reality.[37] That is why you cannot believe everything you read, hear or see: it may be an illusion. There are illusions that amaze, cheer or excite us. There are illusions that hypnotize us and take control of our fingers, forcing us to share that fascinating "fake news" we got on our cell phone with all of our "friends," only to end up making them participants in the same game of illusion that has captured us.

The irony is that in spite of the extensive studies done on speculation and collective illusion, it seems the prince of darkness continues to toy with our deepest human emotions, tempting us to squander our resources on casinos, risky bets, and absurd business ideas.

We get even excited about political-economic ideas. While it is true that neoliberalism can be positive for the macroeconomy, it also cuts social benefits. In contrast, socialism increases social

---

37 "Illusion." Encyclopædia Britannica. Encyclopædia Britannica, inc. Accessed November 16, 2020. http://www. britannica.com/topic/illusion.

benefits, but by choking the middle class with taxes. In the end, the midpoint for Western democracies seems to be populism, the same populism that creates the illusion that social benefits can be maintained without paying the political price of raising taxes. The same populism capable of hypnotizing more than 300 million American citizens and plunging them into an indebtedness of astronomical proportions, as recorded on the website https://usdebtclock.org/.[38]

The American astrophysicist Carl Sagan said that the origins of science and religion are similar. Both seek to fill in the blanks in our knowledge and provide explanations—explanations that must be found at any cost—in the process we call The Search for Truth. Our thinking does not allow us to leave blank spaces around any idea. And this is precisely where the power of magic, the afterlife, extraterrestrials and monsters under the bed comes into play, sealing the marriage between our superstitious beliefs and the illusions spawned by our most far-fetched interpretations of reality. Of course, all of this will lead to new speculation.

The big problem is that it is easier to believe than to not believe. Not believing involves questioning, which requires additional mental effort and energy consumption. Such effort is not pleasant for the metabolic economy of our cells, programmed to save energy. It is easier to avoid the suffering caused by the depletion of energy inherent to the reasoning process.

---

38 U.S. National Debt Clock : Real Time. Accessed November 16, 2020. https://usdebtclock.org/.

Superstition, on the other hand, is the easiest and fastest way to fill in the blanks without the hassle of thinking. We weave superstitions around the stock market, health, extraterrestrial life, death, love, etc.

To make matters worse, beliefs are not the only thing that can cause us to lose our way; there is bad news for the most devout disciples of reason as well. Logical reasoning can also lead to incorrect conclusions. In the set of variables that surround a given situation, there may be confounding variables that cause us to move away from a correct interpretation of reality, or to simply hold the deepest conviction that our illusion is reality. We see this happening all the time, even among the most sophisticated marketing professionals and political scientists. We have already explored how feedback within a group of people with similar illusions can lead the entire group to the firm belief that their misconception is reality (groupthink).

As technology has become our closest companion in good times and bad, it is also accompanying us in the creation of collective illusions. So much so, that we build imaginary communities. We know that the sense of cohesion felt by a group of people is often artificial, and facilitated by the media and social networks. This is usually the case even for the most fanatical elements of nationalism. Many times, these imaginary communities become filter bubbles, i.e., virtual communities of individuals with elements in common who share similar information about what they want to hear.[39] In the end, these communities are just another way that we become disconnected from reality.

We encounter filter bubbles all the time on social networks like Twitter, where we get to select who we want to listen to, what information we want to believe, what is right, or what the majority of people are thinking. The phenomenon is interesting, because it shows that we can be so foolish as to create our own illusions and disconnect ourselves from reality without the need of any external manipulation.

Filter bubbles also remind us a lot of groupthink. It is easy to form this kind a bubble by blocking all those who do not think like us on Twitter, or simply by not following them.

In addition to our foolish penchant for creating our own filter bubbles, social networks are highly useful as tools of control. They not only serve to identify, create and mobilize biased groups (on purpose); they are also able to overcome any limit of modern astrophysics by creating a parallel—albeit entirely imaginary—universe.

Illusion, both rational and as a product of superstition, is clearly a villain, but what about belief? It is very difficult to identify a cut-off point that separates believers from non-believers. There are many shades of gray for the many ways of understanding the universe and God. Even among

39 Daley, Beth. "Why Social Media May Not Be so Good for Democracy." The Conversation, April 15, 2020. https://theconversation.com/why-social-media-may-not-be-so-good-for-democracy-86285.

clergy there are all kinds of contradictions. Although Catholic priest Georges Lemaître was the first to propose the Big Bang theory, there are sectors within the Catholic Church that oppose it to this day. There are also many shades of gray in everything related to human thought. If we ask a group of highly religious people about their concept of God, we will notice that there is no uniformity in their answers. Similarly, if we question a group of atheists about supernatural forces and conspiracy theories, we will find a wide range of beliefs situated along the most absurd and ridiculous lines of traditional ignorance.

This reminds me of a good friend who says he does not believe in religion because it is mass manipulation. Nevertheless, he is capable of weaving all kinds of fantastic tales around both scientific and non-scientific information, deftly reconciling concepts as disparate as the latest theory of quantum physics, conspiracy theories, advances in genetic engineering, and the boogeyman; or making the most childish tales of goblins shake hands with Newton's laws. Apparently, believing or not believing in something specific is not synonymous with mental structuring to seek the truth by the scientific method.

On the brain itself

Human thought is the product of complex chemical and bioelectrical interactions, all regulated by the expression of our genes. So much so, that even transcendental thought is guided by our genetic load and activity. It has been found that the presence and expression of certain genes can predispose us to a particular temperament and even a way of seeing life or understanding the universe. The VMAT1, 5HT1B, OXTR and DRD2 genes are associated with spirituality, in different ways. The VMAT1 and 5HT1B genes are linked to mood-related spirituality, which helps prevent depression. The OXTR is associated with pro-social behavior and empathy, while the DRD2 gene is associated with a greater capacity for transcendence. Interestingly, the first three genes, without the presence of DRD2, are expressed as secular humanism.[40]

In the end, our way of thinking, remembering and behaving depends on the death and birth of new neurons, together with changes in their interconnection. This process, known as neuronal plasticity, is the architect of the mental "wiring" we carry with us throughout our lives. In the end, we are the product of this wiring, which produces the interactions between our biology and society through processes such as religion, education and upbringing.

The mental wiring that defines our way of thinking can also be altered throughout life. In the military, for example, it is well known how to turn soldiers into serial killers. The performance of a soldier during combat can be diminished by the fear of killing, rather than the

40 Anderson, Micheline R., Lisa Miller, Priya Wickra-maratne, Connie Svob, Zagaa Odgerel, Ruixin Zhao, and Myrna M. Weissman. "Genetic Correlates of Spirituality/Religion and Depression: A Study in Offspring and Grandchildren at High and Low Familial Risk for Depression." *Spirituality in Clinical Practice* 4, no. 1 (2017): 43–63. https://doi.org/10.1037/scp0000125.

fear of death. We all know that a moral principle firmly established in our wiring by our social institutions is the Fifth Commandment of the Judeo-Christian tradition: "Thou shalt not kill." However, the mental rewiring to which a soldier is subjected inhibits his morals, turning him into what, outside of combat conditions, we would call a perfect psychopath. For training, the most effective methods are sought to induce an automatic killing response under certain conditions. This discipline has been professionalized and is known as killology. It can lead to what experienced soldiers describe as follows: "Killing someone can be like saying 'Okay, let's go for pizza.'"[41]

Now, behaviors are not only the product of wiring and rewiring. Feelings of guilt, pity and anger precede the desire for transgression within a group.[42]

On interactions

Anger, in particular, can deepen political divisions and hinder the cooperation that is necessary for the functioning of a society. The irony is that civilians and

41 Haddock, Vicki. "THE SCIENCE OF CREATING KILL-ERS / Human Reluctance to Take a Life Can Be Reversed through Training in the Method Known as Killology." SFGATE. San Francisco Chronicle, January 13, 2012. https://www.sfgate.com/science/article/THE-SCIENCE-OF-CREAT-ING-KILLERS-Human-2514123.php.

42 Shepherd, Lee, Russell Spears, and Antony S.r. Manstead. "'This Will Bring Shame on Our Nation': The Role of Anticipated Group-Based Emotions on Collective Ac-tion." *Journal of Experimental Social Psychology* 49, no. 1 (2013): 42–57. https://doi.org/10.1016/j.jesp.2012.07.011.

politicians capable of inciting anger and encouraging others to take action are seen as admirable within democratic culture.[43]

In any case, whatever the intervention or reason for a certain change in behavior, context must also be taken into account, and the motivations that could change the behavior need to be understood. There is no universal formula that always works. It is important to remember that all behavior is grounded in certain beliefs and a collective morality.[44]

Despite this, there are individuals who have difficulty understanding an act within a context, or dealing with the complexity of all the interactions that converge at a given time. For example, it is known that highly orthodox individuals experience an increase in heart rate when they are exposed to arguments against their beliefs. The open expression of their prejudices allows them to normalize their heart rate again. This pattern is not observed in the less orthodox. The finding explains the reason for visceral discussions between individuals holding extreme positions around issues related not only to

---

43 Huber, Michaela, Leaf Van Boven, Bernadette Park, and William T. Pizzi. "Seeing Red: Anger Increases How Much Republican Identification Predicts Partisan Attitudes and Perceived Polarization." *Plos One* 10, no. 9 (2015). https://doi.org/10.1371/journal.pone.0139193.

44 Shepherd, Lee, Russell Spears, and Antony S.r. Manstead. "'This Will Bring Shame on Our Nation': The Role of Anticipated Group-Based Emotions on Collective Action." *Journal of Experimental Social Psychology* 49, no. 1 (2013): 42–57. https://doi.org/10.1016/j.jesp.2012.07.011.

religion, but also to topics such as migration, taxes, social benefits, economic policy, etc.[45]

On good and evil

It is precisely the collective morality that likes to point fingers, defining the good and the bad without taking into account the context or the motivations behind the behaviors it presumes to judge.

As psychologist Ervin Staub has observed, "Evil that arises out of ordinary thinking and is committed by ordinary people is the norm, not the exception."

An example of how ordinary the "bad guys" can be (not to mention how bad we ordinary people can become) can be found in the psychological study of terrorists. Terrorism is the product of people with a normal psychology (like you and me, dear reader), with the difference that their environment and motivations are more complicated. The psychology of terrorists encompasses everything from intrapersonal aspects to ideologies. Despite the complexity of the issue, politicians present it as a temporary problem that fades under the illusion that it is being addressed. In the end, it becomes a distractor from other, more dangerous problems[46].

———————

45 Kossowska, Małgorzata, Paulina Szwed, Aneta Czernatowicz-Kukuczka, Maciek Sekerdej, and Miroslaw Wyczesany. "From Threat to Relief: Expressing Prejudice toward Atheists as a Self-Regulatory Strategy Protecting the Religious Orthodox from Threat." *Frontiers in Psychology* 8 (2017). https://doi.org/10.3389/fpsyg.2017.00873.

46   Arciszewski Thomas, Verlhiac Jean-François, Goncalves Isabelle *et al.*, « From psychology

Now, whatever the wiring, the environment, or the motivation, we can be sure that acts of evil will be more pronounced when they are accompanied by asymmetry in a power relationship (implying disadvantaged victims such as women, children, migrants, poor, indigenous, homosexual, disabled, sick, elderly, etc.), anonymity, turmoil, or dehumanization of the victim. This cocktail can make normal people act in a truly monstrous way.

Such monstrosity not only has an origin: it has also developed tools of self-perpetuation. Perhaps one of the most useful tools it draws on is infiltration, as we will see in the next chapter.

In the end, we all have the capability of being bad or even monstrous at some point. All that is needed are the right circumstances.

of terrorists to psychology of terrorism », *Revue internationale de psychologie sociale*, 2009/3 (Tome 22), p. 5-34. URL : https://www.cairn-int.info/revue-internationale-de-psychologie-sociale-2009-3-page-5.htm

Chapter 8:
Infiltration

*"It is impossible to correct abuses unless we
know that they are going on."*

— Julian Assange

I remember reading an article a while back about the search for black holes in space. I found it interesting that the challenge in their detection is due precisely to their high density, which does not allow light to escape. And so, philosophizing a little, it occurred to me that being the most dense, or the most intense, does not necessarily make something the most obvious. Human societies are part of the same universe, subject to the same laws. If we were to make a pseudoscientific extrapolation, we might be led to think that the most intense social movements are not necessarily the most visible. This line of thinking could easily devolve into conspiracy theories without any objective foundation. Logic does not always lead us to the truth; neither does pseudoscience.

The truth is that we are surrounded by things that our senses are unable to detect, including the movement of political and social game pieces. We depend on information, provided by either our senses or technology, to dimension reality and the events that shape it. However, there are ways we can be deceived or deprived of access to information.

This chapter is precisely about what is not obvious to us. It is not about kings, but about those who maintain close ties to the throne. It is about the cards that are passed under the table, about those who whisper in the ear of the powerful and move the game pieces without taking responsibility for the consequences. Naturally, it is also about those who pull the strings but are nowhere to be found in the history books. It is about infiltration, which is used to attack in the way that submarines and aircraft invisible to radar do. It is about what is not seen and moves revolutions from within. It is about the sphere where thinkers and masterminds are most relevant, but where opportunists and all kinds of sinister types also thrive.

Infiltration is understood as the movement by which water flows through each small pore, each tiny gap between dust and stones, on its virtually unstoppable journey from the surface of the ground to the depths of the earth. This definition, referring to the passage of water through the ground, helps us better understand the concept of how small water molecules can penetrate a great thickness and reach a depth that we could only achieve through immense effort. Just as water penetrates the ground silently and secretly, there are also individuals who penetrate the defenses of a group of which they are part, to obtain information or to exert some kind of influence on the thinking or behavior of the other members.[47]

On certain occasions, infiltration may be accompanied by exfiltration, which is the unauthorized extrusion, exportation or transfer of information from one unit to another (or from one computer to another). The process can be manual, in the case of physical access to information, or it can be automated, through malicious programs present in a network.[48]

An important goal of infiltration is to obtain intelligence information. Intelligence, in government and military operations, evaluates information about the strengths, activities and probable actions of other countries or non-state actors, who are usually enemies or opponents. The term also refers to the collection, analysis, and distribution of such information for covert actions (secret intervention in political or economic matters of other countries). Intelligence is a core part of the power of a nation and essential for decision-making on matters of national security, defense and international politics.[49]

---

47 Meaning of INFILTRATION in the English Cambridge Dictionary. Accessed November 16, 2020. https://dictionary.cambridge.org/es/diccionario/ingles/infiltration.

48 Lord, Nate. "What Is Data Exfiltration?" Digital Guardian, September 11, 2018. https://digitalguardian.com/blog/what-data-exfiltration.

49 "Intelligence." Encyclopædia Britannica. Encyclopædia Britannica, inc. Accessed November 16, 2020. https://www.britannica.com/topic/intelligence-international-relations.

Espionage, on the other hand, is the process of obtaining secret information related to the military, police, commerce or any other source, through the activities of spies, secret agents, or illegal monitoring systems. Espionage is different from other forms of intelligence gathering, particularly because of its natural aggressiveness and illegality.[50]

Military infiltration

In military terms, infiltration refers to a maneuver in which the elements of combat are executed within and across enemy territory without detection, in order to occupy the territory or attack an enemy position from behind. Infiltration involves invisible movements, mainly by forces carrying compact, lightweight equipment. The movements are effected through the most vulnerable support positions of the enemy front line, such as command and control, artillery, logistics, and transportation, cutting off the enemy's defense forces.[51]

An epic example of infiltration is the Trojan Horse, a hollow wooden structure built by the Greeks to gain access to the city of Troy during the Trojan War. The Greeks pretended to retreat from battle,

---

50 "Espionage." Encyclopædia Britannica. Ency-clopædia Britannica, inc. Accessed November 16, 2020. https://www.britannica.com/topic/espionage.

51 Sutherland, Rick Baillergeon and John. "Tactics 101 082 – Infiltraton in History and Practice." Armchair General Magazine We Put YOU in Command, March 14, 2013. http://armchairgeneral.com/tactics-101-082-infiltra-ton-in-history-and-practice.htm.

leaving behind a huge wooden horse as an alleged offering to Athena (goddess of war) that would make Troy impenetrable. The horse was taken inside the city. That night, Greek warriors came out of the horse and opened the gates of the city to allow the entry of the rest of their army, which had returned to carry out the surprise attack.[52]

The planning of a military infiltration is done following the same steps used to plan any other operation. The most important thing is to understand the strengths and weaknesses of one's own forces as well as those of the enemy, in order to determine how the element of surprise can be used to achieve the designated goal. In general, certain basic principles are followed. The infiltration forces must be as small as possible and trained together in command and control, but large enough to get themselves out of any trouble they might encounter and complete the assigned mission. The preparation must include detailed coordination of the forces, with a plan that is clearly understood by all units. It must be ensured that they have the necessary equipment to do their job. Both planning and preparation should be supported by continuous reconnaissance and intelligence gathering. A determination must be made of the points where the infiltration forces will assemble or reorganize in the event they have to scatter. In general, the concept is simple: it consists of maneuvering within an area to fulfill an objective, to do "something" and then

---

52 "Trojan Horse." Encyclopædia Britannica. Ency-clopædia Britannica, inc. Accessed November 16, 2020. https://www.britannica.com/topic/Trojan-horse.

maneuver back towards friendly territory.[53]

Long-range surveillance (LRS) teams are trained to perform different types of infiltration and exfiltration (information extraction) operations for various types of missions. Training for this type of operation increases the probability of survival and success of the mission. Among the deployment methods used are amphibious tactics, helicopters, land vehicles, or going on foot.[54]

Today, infiltration is planned with technological tools that complement traditional tactics. For example, in anti-terrorist operations, a fake computer program can be sent to the enemy, forcing him to connect to the internet and reveal his IP address. Exposing the computer's IP address enables a commando to move in for the capture or elimination of the terrorist cell.[55]

----

53 Sutherland, Rick Baillergeon and John. "Tactics 101 082 – Infiltraton in History and Practice." Armchair General Magazine We Put YOU in Command, March 14, 2013. http://armchairgeneral.com/tactics-101-082-infiltra-ton-in-history-and-practice.htm.

54 Pike, John. "Military." FM 7-93 Chptr 6 Infiltration and Exfiltration. Accessed November 16, 2020. https://www.globalsecurity.org/military/library/policy/army/fm/7-93/Ch6.htm.

55 Hinchliffe, Tim, US Intelligence Paranoia Creeps into Tech, Facebook to Rely on Unnamed Third-party Fact Checkers for Fake News says: Google, Udo Ulfkotte, Is Google's hesitance on WikiLeaks' cybersecurity offer due to a technicality or actual CIA involvement? - InfoSecHotSpot says: Ballmer's USAFacts, et al. "Propaganda Wolves in Sheep's Clothing: The Govt Infiltration of US Media." The Sociable, October 3, 2016. https://sociable.co/web/iraq-propaganda-operation-mockingbird/.

Police infiltration

In police terms, infiltration is a resource used when a group is suspected of having connections to subversive or criminal activity. In these cases, undercover police officers approach the suspected group, feigning interest in becoming members with the goal of gathering information about the organization and its activities. Sometimes, infiltrated agents may encourage group members to participate in criminal activity, which makes it easier to formulate charges against individuals and the organization as a whole. It is common practice for infiltrated agents to offer beers, employment, housing, friendship, and even certain drugs, to foster trust within the group they want to infiltrate.

In the 1960s, the FBI used a counter-intelligence program to interfere with dissident groups. It began with the infiltration of the communist party and quickly expanded to include social groups, right-wing extremists, nationalists, and basically any other even remotely radical organization. Recordings, anonymous letters, blackmail, tax audits and anything else that could be done to discredit leaders and create divisions within organizations were used.[56]

Following the terrorist attacks of September 11, 2001, the police have also used infiltration to gain access to the private sphere of activists' sex lives, in order to silence them and gather intelligence that can be used to demonstrate the power of the police to discipline

---

56 "The Sixties. Revolutions." PBS. Public Broadcasting Service. Accessed November 17, 2020. http://www.pbs.org/opb/thesixties/topics/revolution/index.html.

those who would go against them. Furthermore, the psychological effect produced by the feeling of being watched is more powerful than the surveillance per se. Occasionally, infiltration has been used with the excuse of protecting national security and not for police activity as such. On these lines, some governments have developed methods to avoid confrontation on the physical plane by sowing fear and a sense of insecurity among the potentially disruptive population. Of course, victimizing leaders only helps the recruitment and radicalization of agitators.[57]

Political infiltration

Political infiltration, also known as political entryism, is a practice—widely identified as unethical—in which a political party secures the affiliation of one of its adherents in another political group. Political infiltration is done with the intention of spying or sabotaging. The infiltrated individual can assume a position of trust or even be elected to a position of power, giving him access to the planning level within the party. Political infiltration is often associated with illegal activities such as wiretapping. Traditionally, infiltration has been widely used by communist parties to align non-communist parties with the Marxist left. In the United States, there have been sporadic reports of temporary infiltrations in political campaigns. In countries with

---

57 Loadenthal, Michael. "When Cops 'Go Native': Policing Revolution through Sexual Infiltration and Panopticonism." *Critical Studies on Terrorism* 7, no. 1 (2014): 24–42. https://doi.org/10.1080/17539153.2013.877670.

political instability, the infiltration of the ruling party may be the initial preparation for a coup d'etat or the next revolution.[58]

Examples of political infiltration are contained throughout history. One of the best-known cases is that of Adolph Hitler. Hitler worked as a police spy assigned to infiltrate the German Workers Party. What the police did not expect was that Hitler would end up becoming one of the party's foremost leaders, shaping it according to his own objectives until it became the Nazi party. In the end, his infiltration provided him with the tools to develop his oratory abilities and manipulate the German political system.[59]

Political infiltration is also used by totalitarian governments. A well-known example is the infiltration achieved throughout Italy by Mussolini's propaganda, which portrayed his leadership as responsible only for the good things that happened.[60]

I remember participating once in one of numerous demonstrations against some government decision. After a couple of hours of peaceful and even somewhat

---

58 "Political Infiltration." Political infiltration | World Problems & Global Issues | The Encyclopedia of World Problems. Accessed November 17, 2020. http://encyclope-dia.uia.org/en/problem/142378.

59 History.com Editors. "Beer Hall Putsch." History.com. A&E Television Networks, November 9, 2009. http://www.history.com/topics/germany/beer-hall-putsch.

60 "Benito Mussolini Biography: Italian Dictator & Leader of the National Fascist Party." Biographics, July 5, 2018. https://biographics.org/benito-mussolini-biog-raphy-italian-dictator-and-journalist-who-was-the-lead-er-of-the-national-fascist-party/.

silent (not to say boring) protest, a guy appeared with a bag full of fliers, noise-makers, and a megaphone. The striking thing was that the guy behaved like a professional. He already knew what he was going to shout, displaying all the energy, ease and skill of a major league cheerleader. The guy was inciting the demonstrators and urging them to close the street. He had really done his homework on what would inflame the crowd and raise the temperature of the protest. Fortunately, the gathering remained lively but peaceful until we all retired to our homes. At the time, it seemed like an isolated event. But a couple of years later when the government was defeated by the main opposition party, that same agitator claimed a public office in the new administration. It became clear to me then that he was a political activist from a government opposition party who had infiltrated a protest against a government decision.

Thus, both governments and their opponents compete for the political infiltration of different social groups, or groups with enough muscle to recruit agitators (either to heat things up or to silence them).

In Latin America there is a long history of infiltration. A good example is the Condor plan, which involved a certain amount of intelligence cooperation between dictatorships in Latin America and the United States in order to contain socialist progress in the region.[61]

---

61 Americas, Inside Story. "Tracing the Shadows of 'Operation Condor'." Bolivia | Al Jazeera. Al Jazeera, March 6, 2013. http://www.aljazeera.com/programmes/insidesto-ryamericas/2013/03/2013367461442124.html.

Another good example is Cuba's infiltration and takeover of Venezuela's institutions. Cuba, over the course of two decades, has achieved the cultural, political, social and economic infiltration of different sectors in Latin America as a way of expanding its influence as an arm of the Soviet Union, and later of Russia.[62] [63] [64]

Other forms of infiltration

Cordell Hull, the US Secretary of State during World War II, expressed his fear that the dangers confronting the Western Hemisphere went beyond the threat of direct military invasion. The risks, he said, extended to indirect forms, including the organization of political parties and practices such as the purchase or blackmail of adherents, as well as other forms of penetration and dissemination of propaganda.

---

62 Harris, Paul, and Chris McGreal. "How Russian Spies Infiltrated Suburban America." The Guardian. Guardian News and Media, June 30, 2010. http://www.theguardian.com/world/2010/jun/29/russian-spies-suburban-america.

63 Toro, Francisco. "Fidel Castro's Venezuela Obsession." The Washington Post. WP Company, November 26, 2016. http://www.washingtonpost.com/opinions/global-opinions/fidel-castros-venezuela-obsession/2016/11/26/5a-3d3e9c-b405-11e6-8616-52b15787add0_story.html?noredirect=on.

64 El Líbero. "La Estrategia Cubana Para Influir En La Política Interna De Los Países De América Latina." El Líbero. Accessed November 17, 2020. https://ellibero.cl/actualidad/la-estrategia-cubana-para-influir-en-la-politica-interna-de-los-paises-de-america-latina/.

In other words, infiltration is not exclusively a military, police or political issue. Infiltration through propaganda is widely practiced by power groups, even in Western democracies. The media makes public personalities appear and disappear at their whim.

Propaganda is used to affect the actions and policies of the enemy, either by suppressing material that could be used by the enemy as propaganda, disseminating propaganda that leads a target group to a certain conclusion, leading the enemy to reveal information about himself, or leading the enemy to perform an activity that could discredit him.[65]

An intelligence report prepared by the United States Central Intelligence Agency (CIA) in 1950 details how indoctrination was used by the communist party of former Czechoslovakia. The indoctrination was widely infiltrated in educational institutions at all levels—primary, secondary and even higher education —in order to introduce young people to communist ideology. In the process, students were instilled with a devotion to the communist program and enmity towards certain social classes and capitalist countries. The

---

65 Hinchliffe, Tim, US Intelligence Paranoia Creeps into Tech, Facebook to Rely on Unnamed Third-party Fact Checkers for Fake News says: Google, Udo Ulfkotte, Is Google's hesitance on WikiLeaks' cybersecurity offer due to a technicality or actual CIA involvement? - InfoSecHotSpot says: Ballmer's USAFacts, et al. "Propaganda Wolves in Sheep's Clothing: The Govt Infiltration of US Media." The Sociable, October 3, 2016. https://sociable.co/web/iraq-propaganda-operation-mockingbird/.

communist party also made efforts to infiltrate all potential resistance groups.[66]

If George Orwell's famous novel *1984* (written in the 1940's) portrayed a chilling future of press control, current technologies make child's play of this storyline and the terror it caused in the imaginations of that time. An example of this can be found in Russia's cyber infiltration capabilities. In 2018, there was talk that Russian hackers had infiltrated US power stations to produce blackouts and generate chaos.[67]

Infiltration has also been widely used by the West. During the Cold War, the administration of President Eisenhower understood that there were two ways to stop the expansion of the Soviet system. One way was a revolution, imposed by force on an enemy that had began to produce hydrogen bombs and possessed no small amount of military muscle. The other way was to induce an evolution, which would take several decades. In furtherance of this second strategy, a whole propaganda campaign was designed to promote a cultural infiltration that would exploit cultural vulnerabilities in Soviet ideology. The aim of the propaganda was mainly to distance young people from communist ideology by

---

66 Central Intelligence Agency. "Communist Propaganda, Indoctrination and Infiltration Tactics/Price." *CIA*, Central Intelligence Agency, 20 Mar. 1950, www.cia.gov/library/readingroom/docs/CIA-RDP80-00926A001900040006-3.pdf. Accessed 19 Oct. 2019.

67 LeVine, Steve. "Inside Russia's Invasion of the U.S. Electric Grid." Axios, August 5, 2018. https://www.axios.com/russia-united-states-cyber-war-electric-power-grid-cb71f036-1ccc-47a2-93b7-fe4220e36622.html.

creating contact between young people living under communism and the West. The campaign, which was also heavily implemented in developing countries, sought to change concepts distorted by indoctrination and equip certain social groups with reformist ideas. The fact that Soviet president Nikita Khrushchev recognized the economic damage caused by isolation was used to infiltrate the channels of aperture that were beginning to be permitted.[68]

In 1976, Senator Frank Church wrote that the Central Intelligence Agency (CIA) maintained a network of several hundred foreigners providing intelligence information and influencing public opinion through covert propaganda. These individuals gave the CIA direct access to numerous media and news agencies. Today, infiltration of the media has been facilitated by mergers in the industry, which have reduced the number of economic groups or companies with access to the media and consolidated control over the industry.[69]

As recently as 2019 there have also been reports

---

68 Schwartz, Lowell H. "Cultural Infiltration: A New Propaganda Strategy for a New Era of Soviet—West Relations." *Political Warfare against the Kremlin*, 2009, 181–208. https://doi.org/10.1057/9780230236936_8.

69 Hinchliffe, Tim, US Intelligence Paranoia Creeps into Tech, Facebook to Rely on Unnamed Third-party Fact Checkers for Fake News says: Google, Udo Ulfkotte, Is Google's hesitance on WikiLeaks' cybersecurity offer due to a technicality or actual CIA involvement? - InfoSecHotSpot says: Ballmer's USAFacts, et al. "Propaganda Wolves in Sheep's Clothing: The Govt Infiltration of US Media." The sociable, October 3, 2016. https://sociable.co/web/iraq-propaganda-operation-mockingbird/.

of Washington's plans to establish an infiltration and propaganda machine to separate Moscow from the countries of the Caucasus and Central Asia.[70]

The United States government even has a history of infiltrating the media within its own country. It is estimated that the US government paid around $500 million to a British firm for a campaign to spread false news about Iraq, according to the Bureau of Investigative Journalism. This type of practice, as we know, compromises the freedom of the press and creates a dilemma, since the authorities responsible for maintaining order are precisely the ones committing such ethically questionable acts. When intelligence agencies pose as journalists, they also compromise the credibility of the press as a source of real information.

If we are going to talk about penetration through cultural infiltration, the main actors of the Cold War are not the only experts at this game. A report by the investigative body of the US Senate indicated that as of February 2019, China had penetrated the American education system—from kindergarten to university level—through monetary programs and schemes to indoctrinate American children and youth with communist government propaganda in the classroom. Another report from the Senate Committee on Homeland Security indicated that China had spent $200 million in educational centers known as "Confucius Institutes" to

70 "Washington Reported to Set up Propaganda, Infiltration Machinery to Influence Elections, Drive Wigs between Moscow, Central Asia/Caucasus." *Newslinetj.Com*, 2019, www.newslinetj.com/article/763758/

indoctrinate American students and garner sympathy for the Chinese communist government. While these centers focus expressly on cultural issues and language learning, it would seem their hidden agenda is to change people's views on China in terms of sensitive issues such as Human Rights violations and economic policy.[71]

The *Homeland Security News Wire* also reported in 2018 that China was wielding its powerful influence over US institutions in corrupt ways, with the goal of achieving global hegemony.[72]

Governments and subversives are not the only ones who infiltrate. Money laundering is the process in which the profits from illegal activities are moved around to mislead the authorities, so that they can be enjoyed by criminals without obvious evidence of their origin. A 2009 report estimated that 3.6 percent of the gross world product (GWP) came from criminal activity, and that 2.7 percent of the GWP was laundered. The money is invested in funds, real estate, stocks, and different types of businesses. Usually, the money is moved to countries with stable financial systems but poor structures for the detection of money laundering.

---

71 Author, Alternate. "Propaganda Coup: China In-filtration Into U.S. Education System." Technocracy News, February 28, 2019. http://www.technocracy.news/propa-ganda-coup-china-infiltration-into-u-s-education-system/.

72 "China, Chinese Sharp Power, Chinese Infiltration of U.S.: Homeland Security Newswire." China, Chinese sharp power, Chinese infiltration of U.S. | Homeland Security Newswire, December 21, 2018. http://www.homelandsecu-ritynewswire.com/dr20181221-china-exerting-sharp-pow-er-influence-on-american-institutions.

There, money launderers infiltrate financial institutions and acquire control of large sectors of the economy, public servants and even governments.[73]

Financial infiltration is not exclusive to criminals. It is also practiced by those with an affinity for power (who are often just successful delinquents). For example, multiple contracts with private companies for public services can be regarded as nothing more than a way to benefit friends and relatives financially with taxpayers' money. Even funds earmarked for technological development are often tied to the capabilities of certain companies that have already infiltrated the decision-making circles.

Examples abound in which a government in one country provides some kind of aid to another country. In reality, what the donor government does is transfer public funds contributed by its taxpayers to companies with which it is connected in some way. It becomes another "legal" and justified way of transferring public money to a company under the pretext of providing aid.

You might think that the influence wielded by the most powerful in the halls of justice is an original sin of capitalism, but you'd be wrong. In his book *Extraordinary Popular Delusions and the Madness of Crowds,* Scottish poet Charles Mackay tells us that in the Middle Ages, the condition of *convicta et combusta* applied mainly to poor, ugly old women accused of witchcraft. Meanwhile, the powerful and their relatives were forgiven of all sorts of crimes, receiving no greater

---

73 "FATF Public Statement - 23 October 2015." Accessed November 17, 2020. http://rbidocs.rbi.org.in/rdocs/content/pdfs/256FATF031215_A1.pdf.

punishment than some laughable fine. And this occurred in primitive and absolute monarchies, which were far from being capitalist.

Simply put, the dark art of going unnoticed is part of life. It accompanies us stealthily at every moment of our daily routine. It is present in every aspect of our environment. It occupies a small space, but with so much density that it sucks up all evidence of its existence, just like the powerful black holes. Whether large or small in scale, infiltrations—military, police, political, propaganda, media, ideological, cultural, institutional, or even financial—have been present in uprisings and conflicts of the past, and will surely be one of the sharp swords that leads the next great revolution.

Once we understand that reality is much harsher than fiction and capable of putting our wildest imagination to shame, we can only ask ourselves: Where is humanity headed? Surely we will cause our own extinction, gradually killing ourselves off, just as we have been killing off the ecosystems of the only planet we are able to inhabit at this time. Could it be that in the future, the reign of *homo sapiens* will be relegated to the fossil records of planet Earth, just like the dinosaurs? Except for one big difference: the dinosaurs went extinct due to a convergence of natural causes, while we humans could be extinguished by our own intrinsic stupidity. That is precisely the topic we will be looking at in the next chapter.

Chapter 9:
The human species—on the road to extinction?

"The earth will become a fireball."

— Stephen Hawking

Today, it is not unusual to read numerous predictions about how much time humankind has left before extinction. The forecasts include climate change, population growth, speculation about food shortages, water, etc., not to mention the dark end-times prophecies that have emerged throughout history.

You may well ask yourself what a chapter on human extinction is doing in a book on revolutions.

As we have already seen, great revolutions require a platform for discussion, and the survival of our species on this planet is one of the most controversial and discussed topics of our times. It is at the forefront of arguments between ideological and political currents when facing off in public debate.

Population curves

Before continuing, we must understand that any population can sustain its growth as long as there is a source of nutrients and a way to eliminate toxic waste.

Populations of living beings basically present two types of growth curves. When the birth rate is higher than the death rate, population growth takes the form of a J, representing an exponential increase in number. When a balance is reached between births and deaths and a stable number of individuals is maintained, the curve takes the form of an S.[74]

The J-shaped curve is, in fact, only the first part of the S-shaped growth curve, and varies according to the availability of resources and the life span of organisms.

An example of an S-shaped growth curve can be found in the population dynamics of mice, as illustrated in the following graph:

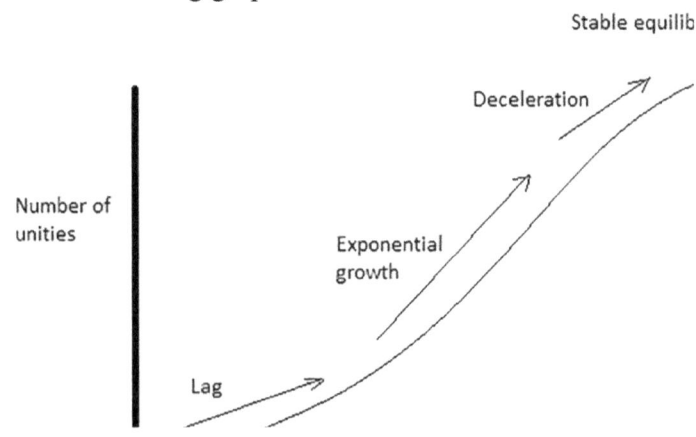

74 "Population Growth Curves: Ecology." Biology Discussion, September 16, 2016. https://www.biology-discussion.com/population/population-growth/population-growth-curves-ecology/51854.

Growth is slow in the initial phase because the first individuals must mature before they can reproduce. In the deceleration phase, the adults start to reach the end of their life cycle and die off. Finally, in the equilibrium phase, the population remains stable because "something" in the environment becomes a limiting factor, be it food, water, predators, diseases, excess toxic waste, etc. (factors associated with population density, as we commonly observe today in our cities). That is, in any population, growth is sustained until resource limitations or other environmental factors intervene.[75]

If a population is unable to achieve a sustainable equilibrium or external factors (such as natural disasters and climate change) break the equilibrium, resources are depleted and disease becomes more widespread, resulting in increased mortality and a subsequent decline in numbers.

Bacteria make an ideal subject for this type of curve, since their life cycle is extremely short, allowing us to observe in a highly abbreviated period what could take years, decades, or even centuries to record for higher orders of animals.

The graph shows the population dynamics for a colony of bacteria in a closed system. The number of units on the vertical axis, vs. time on the horizontal axis.

---

75 "Population Density and Growth." Encyclopædia Britannica. Encyclopædia Britannica, inc. Accessed November 17, 2020. https://www.britannica.com/science/population-ecology/Population-density-and-growth.

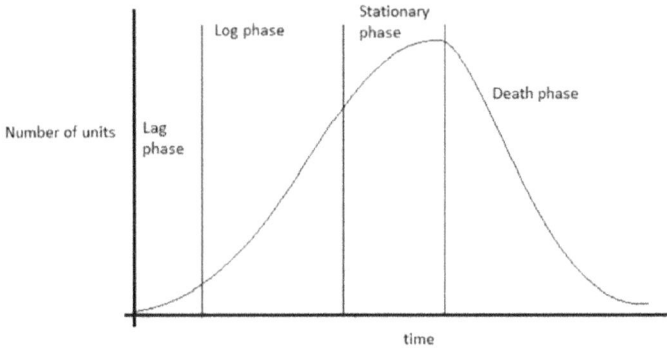

Characteristics of our species

Human conception has been a topic of conversation for millennia, but talk is cheap when you do not have the slightest idea of what you are dealing with. It was not until the end of the nineteenth century that the observations and discoveries of multiple scientists allowed us to understand how the fertilization process occurs, and it was not until the second half of the twentieth century that science really understood the process of embryogenesis with enough certainty to take an active role and proceed with the first *in vitro* fertilizations. Today, *in vitro* fertilizations are seen as quite natural and have become part of everyday life. However, from the time of the first postulations to the first manipulations of embryos, scientists have had to confront myths, fables, and all manner of opposition. Needless to say, there has been no lack of self-anointed prophets proclaiming that the understanding and manipulation of human conception is a sign of the End Times.

We owe our success as a species to our intelligence and to the shape of our hands, equipped with opposable thumbs. Both characteristics have allowed us to make tools and develop technologies in order to transform our environment for our benefit.

There are many theories about the origin of our intelligence, which appears to be closely related to the size of our brain. What is certain is that something happened around two million years ago that caused our brain to increase rapidly in size to what we have today.

The following graph represents cranial volume on the vertical axis, and time on the horizontal axis.

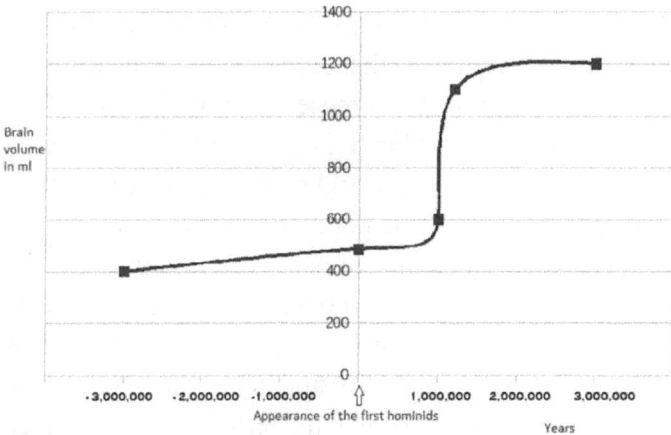

Brain capacity of hominins by time period

On the left is the probable cranial volume at the moment when the common ancestor of chimpanzees and humans diverged. On the central line (point "0"), we find the cranial volume of *Australopithecus africanus*; to the right is the cranial volume of *Homo habilis*, followed by the considerably larger cranial volume of *Homo erectus*, and finally, the average cranial volume of *Homo sapiens*.

We will not enter into the controversies around the cause of such a dramatic change in our intelligence. It is enough to say that this intelligence, together with the characteristics of our limbs and our technology, have altered our population growth curve. This alteration does not exactly coincide with natural changes, however.

The human population curve

As a species, humanity has amassed numerous achievements, such as organizing to hunt, mastering fire, developing agriculture, forming civilizations, and adapting to different habitats. However, it was not until the industrial revolution that our technological advances led to a significant increase in population. More specifically, there has been an exponential acceleration in the growth rate of the world population since 1950, in what can be called a true population explosion.

The causes of this explosion are multiple. On the one hand, there are those who argue that the decrease in the practice of breastfeeding from the 1930s to the 1960s led to an increase in fertility and an accelerated growth rate. More recently, however, the fertility rate has tended to decrease as human development improves. But even though the birth rate has gone down, the population has continued to grow as the mortality rate has declined for all ages, credited in part to the appearance of vaccines, antibiotics and a better understanding of microbiology.

The decrease in mortality has led to a progressive increase in life expectancy. At the time of writing, it is estimated that are as many as 450,000 people over the age of 100 throughout the world. In the United States alone, in 2014 it was estimated that there were 72,197 people over 100 years of age.[76] While the proportion of centenarians is slowly increasing, governments are lagging behind in the development of public policies to deal with the changing demographics.

Let's look at the growth curve of the human population over the last twelve thousand years.

Human population in the last 12,000 years

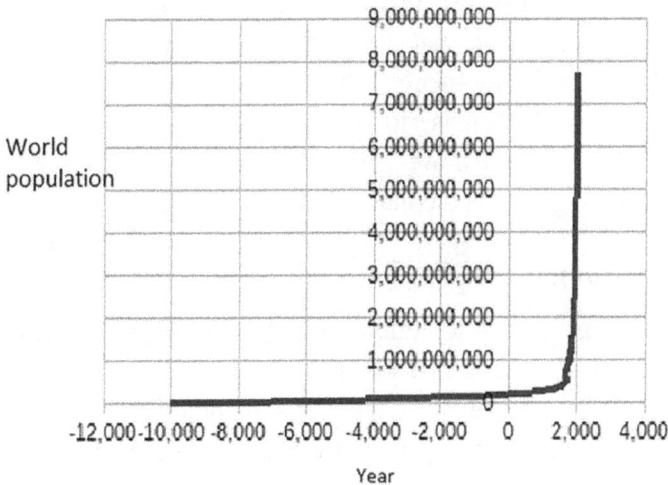

We know that the rise of the curve will not be infinite. There are a variety of factors that have been affecting the human population curve in different ways.

---

76   Fessenden, Marissa. "There Are Now More Americans Over Age 100 and They're Living Longer Than Ever." Smithsonian.com. Smithsonian Institution, January 22, 2016. http://www.smithsonianmag.com/smart-news/there-are-more-americans-over-age-100-now-and-they-are-living-longer-180957914/.

Some make the ascent more pronounced, others make it less pronounced. If the environment remains stable, the population will reach a plateau, which by some estimates will occur at around 11 billion inhabitants. But we know that sooner or later, population size will decrease due to resource shortages, epidemics, or difficulty dealing with toxic waste. The only thing our technology does is delay the arrival at an inevitable point of balance and descent.[77]

Population growth curves are also altered by migration. However, this point is irrelevant on a global scale, considering that the earth's biosphere as a closed system. At the moment we humans have nowhere else to go. And while there is a lot of talk about space colonization, we do not know if we will ever have the technology or wealth to go out and conquer another planet.

How long do we live?

Before going out to conquer another planet, it would be interesting to contrast our notion of who we think we are with what we are in the real scheme of things.

Life expectancy at birth has been increasing. The ceiling on human lifespan has been determined to be 125 years.[78] At least, our biology seems to have set it at that number.

---

77 "The Future of the World's Population in 4 Charts." World Bank Blogs. Accessed November 17, 2020. https://blogs.worldbank.org/opendata/future-world-s-population-4-charts.

78 "Maximum Human Lifespan Has Already Been Reached." ScienceDaily. ScienceDaily, October 5, 2016. http://www.sciencedaily.com/releases/2016/10/161005132823.htm.

However, man is pretentious in his actions and thought, as if he had always been on the planet. Modern humans have only been around for 65,000 of Earth's 4,500 million years. The universe is probably 13,000 million years old. That means that humanity has existed for only 1/69,230 of the planet's existence, and 1/200,000 of the universe's existence. If life on the planet appeared 3.5 billion years ago, then modern humans have lived for only 1/53,846 of that time. If you live to 100, you will have lived 1/650 of the time that modern humans have been on the planet, but only 1/35,000,000 of the time that there has been life on the planet. At 100 years of age, you will have lived only 1/10,000,000 of the time from our planet's formation to the appearance of the first life forms.

Like mosquitoes

To put things in perspective, a female mosquito lives on average seven weeks. That is 1/742 of the life of a 100-year-old human. In other words, if you reach 100, the ratio of your life to the time modern humans have been present on earth is only a little more than the ratio of the average female mosquito's life to yours. On your 100th birthday, proportionally, if you were the planet, humanity would only have accompanied you for the last 12 hours. Your 100 years of life are almost 60,000 times more ephemeral for the planet than the mosquito's life is for you. That is, 100 years are to the earth what one measly minute is to you.

To look at it another way, sturgeon fish have lived on the earth for 200 million years. That is 3,000 times longer than modern humans. If non-avian dinosaurs lived for 179 million years, modern humans have been present on the planet barely 1/2,753 of that time.

It is no less absurd to compare ourselves as individuals against our own species. If each of us is one-in-seven billion, meaning that within our species, we stand out about as much as half a second does in a life of 100 years, or as a seventh of a gram does within a ton. We tend to make ourselves believe that we are unique, but in reality, our "weight" as part of the total world population is equivalent to just one-seventh of the weight of one grain in a kilo of sugar. If humanity were the Pan-American Highway, each of us would correspond to just 6.8 millimeters of its 30,000 miles.

Even in terms of our own biology, the figures are no less impressive. Your father probably produced 525 billion sperm throughout his life, of which at least 40 million competed at the same time to fertilize just one of the one million eggs with which a woman is born. This means that the probability of having the genetic code that makes you who you are is no more than one-in-eighty trillion at the time of fertilization, and no more than one-in-twenty quintillion throughout life.

Talking about the probability of life, our sun is only one of 100,000 million stars in an average-sized galaxy, and our galaxy is only one of 10,000 million galaxies in the observable universe. Literally speaking, our sun is to all the other stars what a single grain of sand is to all the sand on planet Earth.[79]

79 "About How Many Stars Are in Space?" UCSB Science Line. Accessed November 17, 2020. http://scienceline.ucsb.edu/getkey.php?key=3775.

Today we know that the presence of planets is common in our galaxy. Extrapolating what was observed by the Kepler space telescope, there are scientists who estimate that in our galaxy there may be 500 million planets at the right distance from their "sun" to allow for the existence of liquid water (necessary for life). However, this estimate does not contemplate mass, density, or atmospheric composition. In addition, only 10 percent of the galaxy has the characteristics to accommodate life, and it is not exactly where the highest concentration of stars is found.[80]

Having the right characteristics does not mean that there is life on all or even most of these planets, with civilizations of big-headed men who communicate by telepathy. Recall that our species has only been present for 1/69,230 of the total existence of the planet, and the question of our permanence is the reason for this chapter. In fact, just learning to write took our species at least 60,000 years.

Finally, while the probability of intelligent extraterrestrial life is real, it is not as high as we might think, in light of all the factors that have to coincide at a given time. Something equivalent to the entire series of phenomena that gave rise to life on Earth would have to occur. Furthermore, the planet's solar system must be in the stage of its life cycle that makes this possible, and there must have been sufficient opportunity for life to evolve in a manner similar to ours.

---

80 John P. Millis, Ph.D. "Astronomers Want to Know about Habitable Planets." ThoughtCo. Accessed November 17, 2020. http://www.thoughtco.com/counting-habitable-planets-3072596.

In summary, our dreams of escaping our planet's closed biological system will probably have to wait a little longer.

Repeat Extinctions

Although it may trouble us to think that our species could go extinct, we must not forget that the planet has already gone through five mass extinctions. Some scholars affirm that the current rate at which species are disappearing places us in a sixth mass extinction. The truth is that 90 percent of the species that have inhabited the earth are extinct. The possible causes range from the impact of an asteroid in the most recent event, which ended the age of the dinosaurs, to massive volcanic eruptions 250 million years ago that eradicated more than 90 percent of species, as well as massive glaciations that lowered the sea level 440 million years ago. The other two events were one of undetermined cause 200 million years ago, and the die-off of 70 percent of marine life 360 million years ago.[81] [82]

At the time of writing, scholars from the University of New York and Nanjing have suggested that the so-called "Guadalupian extinction" was another mass

---

81   Michael Greshko and National Geographic Staff. "What Are Mass Extinctions, and What Causes Them?" Mass extinction facts and information from National Geographic, September 26, 2019. http://www.nationalgeo-graphic.com/science/prehistoric-world/mass-extinction/.

82   Richter, Viviane. "The Big Five Mass Extinctions." Cosmos Magazine, October 27, 2020. https://cosmosmaga-zine.com/palaeontology/big-five-extinctions/.

extinction event 260 million years ago in which 60 percent of marine species disappeared. This coincided with massive eruptions in the Emeishan Traps in southern China, which leads us to believe that there was global warming. Such a discovery positions humans as the cause of the seventh, and not the sixth, mass extinction.[83] [84]

Of course, there are other ways that life on earth could go extinct, including gamma-ray bursts, loss of our magnetic field, the passage of another star through the solar system (it is estimated that certain stars are on a path of potential collision with the sun in the next million years), or the collision of the earth with another planet, among others.[85]

Obviously, we owe much of our presence here to chance, or whatever we want to call it. The game of odds is played on every street corner of existence, in a casino with no exit door.

In fact, it appears that dinosaurs became extinct not so much because of the asteroid's collision with the

83 Georgiou, Aristos. "Seventh Mass Extinction? Severe and Deadly Event 260 Million Years Ago Discovered by Scientists." Newsweek. Newsweek, September 11, 2019. https://www.newsweek.com/seventh-mass-extinction-se-vere-deadly-event-1458474.

84 O'Neill, Mike. "It's Official: Scientists See a 'New' Mass Extinction." SciTechDaily, September 9, 2019. https://scitechdaily.com/its-official-scientists-see-a-new-mass-ex-tinction/.

85 Barras, Colin. "Earth—How Long Will Life Survive on Planet Earth?" BBC. BBC, March 23, 2015. http://www.bbc.co.uk/earth/story/20150323-how-long-will-life-on-earth-last.

earth, but because of the particular site it hit. Even in matters of going extinct, luck plays its hand.[86]

There are aspects that we often overlook in the debate, such as the fact that we exist in a biosphere altered by multiple disasters, the last of which led to the extinction of the dinosaurs. Dr. Ian Hatton of McGill University found that the proportion between predators and prey follows a mathematical relationship and is constant in most ecosystems. For each doubling of the number of prey, the combined mass of predators increases 1.7 times. However, our species developed in an ecosystem that is still suffering from the destruction left by the impact of an asteroid on the Yucatan peninsula 65 million years ago.[87] At that time, it is estimated that around 80 percent of all animal species disappeared.[88] Undoubtedly, this altered the ecosystem and probably tipped the balance in favor of our ancestors by altering the ratio between them, as potential prey, and their natural predators.

---

86   Dijl, Photograph by Martin Van. "Dino-Killing Asteroid Hit Just the Right Spot to Trigger Extinction." National Geographic, November 9, 2017. https://www.nationalgeographic.com/news/2017/11/dinosaurs-extinction-asteroid-chicxulub-soot-earth-science/.

87   St, Nicholas. "Dinosaurs Might Not Be Extinct Had the Asteroid Struck Elsewhere." The New York Times. The New York Times, November 9, 2017. https://www.nytimes.com/2017/11/09/science/dinosaurs-asteroid-chicxulub-extinction.html.

88   "K–T Extinction." Encyclopædia Britannica. Encyclopædia Britannica, inc. Accessed November 17, 2020. http://www.britannica.com/science/K-T-extinction.

Our extinction

To live, by definition, is to be born, grow, reproduce and die. Something immortal cannot be alive, and something alive cannot be eternal.

Is the world going to end? Matter is not created or destroyed, it is simply transformed. It is estimated that our planet can accommodate life for about another 1.7 billion years.[89] However, it is expected that in one billion years, the sun's life cycle as a star will cause it to expand until all liquid water on planet Earth evaporates; in five billion years, the sun is expected to swallow our planet.

Is the human species going to end? Certainly, we will all disappear as individuals, but it also expected that at some point we will become extinct as a species. We have no choice but to surrender to the hand of fate. In fact, the acceptance of fate is part of our ability to adapt as individuals and as a species. It is part of the positive mentality which has allowed us to survive, what we often call the will of God.

We might evolve into something more terrible. Who is to say? Perhaps into a type of creature that will regard us in the same way we now regard *Australopithecus.* Or we will simply disappear, not because of the harm we have caused to the environment, but by an asteroid or massive volcanic eruptions, or some other type of natural phenomenon. We could become extinct just as

_____

89 Parry, Wynne. "How Much Longer Can Earth Support Life?" LiveScience. Purch, September 18, 2013. http://www.livescience.com/39775-how-long-can-earth-support-life.html.

90 percent of the species that have inhabited the planet in the past did.

Extinction by our own hand

Of course, it is more likely that other species of living beings will go extinct first, not so much because of our great capacity for adaptation, boldness and intelligence, but because of the sovereign degree of idiocy we demonstrate each time we come up with some crazy new way to live more comfortably and less accompanied.

It is here where another concern related to humankind's survival of on earth arises: climate change. Professor Daniel Rothman of MIT has calculated that by 2100, the planet could cross the threshold of CO_2-induced climate change and enter the sixth mass extinction event.

Our intelligence has reached its maximum point of brightness with the ironic twist that the most intelligent species on the planet uses its technology, which has taken centuries to develop, for something as silly as inventing intelligent machines to kill each other.

In 2017, *The Telegraph* published an article stating that there are an estimated 15,000 nuclear warheads in the world, of which 10,000 are in service.[90]

According to the Global Challenges Foundation, while a nuclear war between the United States and

---

90 Kirk, Ashley. "How Many Nukes Are in the World and What Could They Destroy?" The Telegraph. Telegraph Media Group, July 4, 2017. http://www.telegraph.co.uk/news/0/many-nukes-world-could-destroy/.

Russia would cause terrible devastation, the main cause for concern would be the subsequent nuclear winter, during which an 8-degree drop in the planet's temperature could be expected.[91]

As much as the idea of nuclear war terrifies us, we must not forget that nature is not always delicate and that the amounts of energy it is capable of releasing can absolutely overwhelm the fragility of life. The eruption of Mount St. Helens is just such an example: in 1980, it released energy equivalent to 1,600 nuclear bombs.[92] Meanwhile, a hurricane can release the equivalent of up to 10,000 nuclear bombs along its path.[93]

In fact, the 2004 earthquake on the island of Sumatra, with a magnitude of 9.1, released the equivalent of 23,000 nuclear bombs like the one dropped on Hiroshima.[94]

91 Higgins, Abigail. "10 Ways the World Is Most Likely to End, Explained by Scientists." Vox. Vox, October 18, 2018. http://www.vox.com/future-perfect/2018/10/18/17957162/nuclear-war-asteroid-volcano-science-climate-change.

92 Contributors, HowStuffWorks.com. "How Much Energy in a Hurricane, a Volcano, and an Earthquake?" HowStuffWorks Science. HowStuffWorks, January 27, 2020. https://science.howstuffworks.com/environmental/energy/energy-hurricane-volcano-earthquake2.htm.

93 "Hurricanes: The Greatest Storms on Earth." NASA. NASA. Accessed November 17, 2020. https://earthobservatory.nasa.gov/features/Hurricanes.

94 France 24. "When Tsunamis Strike: Five Deadliest Disasters." France 24. France 24, September 29, 2018. http://www.france24.com/en/20180929-when-tsunamis-strike-five-deadliest-disasters.

It has been estimated that the impact of the asteroid that led to the extinction of the dinosaurs released energy equivalent to a whopping 100 million atomic bombs. That is what it takes to leave a 180-kilometer-wide scar like the Chicxulub crater on Mexico's Yucatan Peninsula,[95] with the beautiful caves that tourists enjoy today.

In short, no matter how much we spend on weapons, our ability to destroy is put to shame by Mother Nature.

Or to put it another way, it is unlikely that our extinction will be due directly to a shortage of resources or excess of waste. These two factors could reduce our population, but not make us disappear altogether. It is even unlikely that we will be annihilated by a nuclear war.

Nevertheless, it is to be expected that the issue of human survival will be the subject of revolutions in the future, for many reasons. These range from the struggle for resources that will become proportionately scarcer, to struggles for ways to deal with our industrial waste. The alterations we make in our environment trigger changes that affect everything from demographic dynamics to the size of economies, which in turn can affect the population balance in different countries and regions.

Without a doubt, the most important revolution we need to promote is one of reflecting on our inherent fragility, egotism and foolishness as a species.

_____

95   Fleur, Nicholas St. "Drilling Into the Chicxulub Crater, Ground Zero of the Dinosaur Extinction (Published 2016)." The New York Times. The New York Times, November 17, 2016. http://www.nytimes.com/2016/11/18/science/chicxulub-crater-dinosaur-extinction.html.

Chapter 10:
Heading for Another World War

"When diplomacy ends, war begins."
— *Adolf Hitler*

Many things in life are not easy to understand. But rationalizing the act of murder to the point that it becomes legal and ethically acceptable, on the pretext that the victims are enemies of the homeland, the nation, or its citizens? Viewed dispassionately, that's what war is about.

War has accompanied us throughout our existence as a species, along with all sorts of other foolish things we've managed to do, such as polluting our own environment and messing up the climate of the only planet we are able inhabit at this time.

War is so innate to humanity that it is impossible to contemplate our fragility as a species without associating it with acts as senseless as war.[96] It has played a part

---

96 Tzabar, Rami. "Earth—Do Chimpanzee Wars Prove That Violence Is Innate?" BBC. BBC, August 11, 2015. http://www.bbc.com/earth/story/20150811-do-animals-fight-wars.

in many social changes and upheavals, representing a decisive element in the course of some of the greatest revolutions.

This chapter brings together facts and opinions that may not be liked by all readers, but I invite you to take part in the exercise of thinking together with due respect for different opinions and points of view. First, let's examine this question:

Are we heading towards more peace or more violence?

There are times when we get the impression that we are approaching the end times, the apocalypse or the great Armageddon that will bring an end to all things. We seem to live in a world devoid of values, on a path of self-destruction leading to the final judgment. Such thinking is questionable. It could be the product of a biased perception due to our prejudices and the media coverage given to acts of violence, or it could be simply a product of the psychological trauma induced by news of dubious intellectual value, with images and videos that reach our smartphones almost instantly.

If we are going to speak with solid arguments, one of the most influential minds on the subject is Harvard psychology professor Steven Pinker. Pinker says the world is becoming less and less violent, after reviewing statistics of genocide, terrorism, homicide and war over the years. He affirms that violent events as a whole have been drastically declining over the last decades. The reason for such a change? We'll probably never know for sure. The first thing that comes to mind is that international cooperation and commercial networks have made it more profitable to trade than to go to war.[97] [98]

Pinker's optimistic view seems to be shared by the Uppsala Conflict Data Program. The program recorded 254 armed conflicts between 1946 and 2018, of which 114 were classified as wars. The number of conflicts appears to have decreased since the Cold War. The big question we must ask is: To what extent is this reduction a product of the strengthening of a culture of peace among decision makers? Is it not, rather, the product of the power vacuum that remained after the collapse of communism, in what appeared to be a unipolar world? Will the arms race we are witnessing in recent years lead to new armed conflicts between competitors? Or will the world remain less violent thanks to all the lessons we have learned on how to end conflicts and negotiate with greater skill?

University of Oxford economist Max Roser and his team of researchers reviewed the figures for victims of armed conflict starting in the year 1400 and found that the rate has ranged between one and almost 200 deaths per 100,000 inhabitants. The oscillations have become increasingly marked, resulting in a generally

---

97 "Despite The Headlines, Steven Pinker Says The World Is Becoming Less Violent." NPR. NPR, July 16, 2016. http://www.npr.org/2016/07/16/486311030/despite-the-headlines-steven-pinker-says-the-world-is-becoming-less-violent.

98 "No, The World Isn't Getting More Violent, Here's Why." unilad. Accessed November 17, 2020. http://www.unilad.co.uk/featured/is-the-world-becoming-more-violent/.

ascending line despite the fact that deaths from armed conflicts have shown a dramatic decline since World War II. They also found that conflicts between major powers have been declining in the last 500 years. Similarly, deaths from armed conflicts are less and less attributable to conflicts between nations.

In another study, University of Notre Dame anthropologist Rahul Oka led a team of scholars who researched hundreds of societies and battles, comparing the total population, fighting capacity, army size and casualty rates. The team found that the larger the populations have been, the lower the proportionate casualty rate.[99] Thus, the proportionate decrease in victims of violence observed by Pinker seems to be simply a natural statistical consequence of a larger population inhabiting the same planet.

Another possible explanation is that the forms of violence have been changing throughout history. It is only natural that acts of aggression take different forms in keeping with changes in the environment and circumstances, and it can be argued that it is not appropriate to compare the types of violence that occurred 100 years ago with those we see today on our

---

99 Michael PriceDec. 15, 2017, 2020 Jocelyn KaiserNov. 16, 2020 Jon CohenNov. 16, 2020 Warren CornwallNov. 13, 2020 Jon CohenNov. 11, 2020 Lucy HicksNov. 11, 2020 Lucy HicksNov. 9, 2020 Lucy HicksOct. 30, 2020 Robert F. ServiceOct. 22, and 2020 Lucy HicksOct. 20. "Why Human Society Isn't More-or Less-Violent than in the Past." Science, December 19, 2017. http://www.sciencemag.org/news/2017/12/why-human-society-isn-t-more-or-less-violent-past.

streets. An assessment of modern forms of violence is provided by the Institute for Economics and Peace (IEP), which stated in its June 2018 report that the world is less peaceful than before. The report mentioned that the situation had improved in 71 countries but worsened in 92, with regard to United Nations peacekeeping efforts, border conflicts, civil wars, and political repression. To reach this determination, an index was used that took into account wars, military budget, imprisonment, political repression, corruption, and relations with bordering countries.[100]

In short, the subject warrants a more thorough discussion in order to analyze and verify the different arguments. It should be noted that media coverage is largely responsible for our perception of the world. We are bombarded on every side by news of homicides, shootings and all kinds of violence, which generates fear, anxiety, and even depression. But the psychological impact does not seem to be taken into account by public policy makers. Everything seems to indicate that the media's claim to free speech is more powerful than any proposal aimed at promoting the collective mental health of our societies.[101]

---

100 Dudley, Dominic. "Where And Why The World Is Getting More Dangerous." Forbes. Forbes Magazine, June 6, 2018. http://www.forbes.com/sites/dominicdudley/2018/06/06/why-the-world-is-getting-more-dangerous/.

101 "Is the Modern World More Violent?" *Psychology Today*, 2015, www.psychologytoday.com/us/blog/the-human-beast/201506/is-the-modern-world-more-violent

Mine for as far as I can see

It is commonly understood that the borders of a territory are established by the ability to defend them from others who may want the territory for themselves. The group of players disputing ownership weave a tangle of relationships in which each represents a threat to others.

This type of entanglement reminds me of the arrival of certain American settlers in the mountains of Chiriqui, a province in western Panama endowed with an abundance of natural beauty including mountain ranges, forests, waterfalls, and beaches. The region's exuberant natural landscapes are equaled only by its colorful tales and anecdotes. The protagonists of these stories, which can still be heard throughout the countryside, are numerous and varied, ranging from the boogeyman, goblins and witches, to American and European settlers from the time of the California gold rush and the early days of the twentieth century. There are countless anecdotes of cowboys who arrived in sparsely populated regions and fell in love with the area's natural beauty. In some cases the adventurers decided to build a cabin, settle down and start a new life on land of their own. Establishing a spread back then was quite easy. It was simply a question of building a house in an unpopulated location and defining the boundaries. The methodology for defining property size was objective, concrete and extremely easy to implement: "It's mine for as far as I can see." Actually, the limits could better be described: "As far as a bullet from my rifle can travel." As with conflicts between countries, struggles began to appear between these cowboys when the sight (or rather, the bullets) of at least two different cowboys hit on the same spot.

The first time I heard such tales I found them hard to believe. I knew that Panama had been marked by the California Gold Rush of the nineteenth century in multiple ways, economically, politically, and culturally. What I had never imagined was that a piece of the American West had landed right in the middle of the mountainous landscapes of my country. Later, I understood that more than making their mark in a remote region, it had been a practice of greed derived from our economic model based on private property and the lack of an institutional structure for maintaining order at that time (a situation that it many ways does not seem to have changed much to this day).

It seems that humanity has not yet reached the level of strength and structuring of its global institutions to prevent the authorities, like the cowboys of more than a century ago, from setting their sights on an area of that is of interest to more than one party. The radius of the military capability of multiple powers overlaps in many areas where it is not only looks that are crossed, but bullets as well.

As could be expected, the cowboys from the time of the gold rush understood that another settler in their field of vision represented a threat to the integrity of their land, however arbitrarily defined. And that is precisely where the concept of "preventive war" comes into play. Like the cowboys, global powers fire the first shot as a warning to defend the integrity of their interests. Preventive wars have been waged time and again throughout history. In them, a power that is for the most part on the decline foresees the damage that could be incurred in a future war with a threatening power that is on the rise, and decides to go to war before the situation continues to deteriorate.[102]

Place your bets

Wars are bets, and while certain aspects can tilt the balance to one side or the other, there will always be unforeseen factors that depend entirely on chance. Military powers are constantly seeking to develop technology that will give them victory over an adversary. Wars are one-time events; there is no such thing as a second chance to see if this time you actually win. For this reason, before embarking on an armed conflict, calculators are brought out in order to estimate the costs and potential opportunities involved. In the words of American Civil War general William Tecumseh Sherman, "War is cruelty... . The crueler it is, the sooner it will be over."

An important factor to take into account in any calculation involving armed conflict is the economic one. Economics move the world, and wars tend to have positive economic effects in the short term. However, studies of the economic consequences of US wars after World War II have found that public debt and taxes increased during most conflicts. It was also found that consumption and investment decreased during

---

102 Levy, Jack S. "Declining Power and the Preventive Motivation for War." *World Politics* 40, no. 1 (1987): 82–107. https://doi.org/10.2307/2010195.

armed conflicts, while inflation increased and high-tech investment shifted to industries related to arms development.[103]

Everything seems to indicate that wars have a predominantly negative impact on the economy of the countries involved. These impacts are both direct and indirect, and include not only the loss of life but also the large number of disabled. Similarly, there are opportunity costs associated with the focus on military spending. It comes as no surprise, then, that regression analysis (a line that relates two variables) has revealed no correlation between war and economic growth. It has also been observed that while military spending increases during war, it does not return to pre-war levels when the conflict ends.[104]

In 2017, the Institute for Economy and Peace (IEP) estimated that the global economic impact of violence was $14.8 trillion ($14,800,000,000,000), equivalent to 12.4 percent of the global gross domestic product. In addition, it was estimated that the most peaceful countries tended to have higher gross domestic products, less inflation, and lower interest rates.

Reports and analyses such as these suggest that the calculations that have led to the most recent wars have

103 Michael Shank, Ph.D. "Economic Consequences of War on U.S. Economy: Debt, Taxes and Inflation Increase; Consumption and Investment Decrease." HuffPost. Huff-Post, April 23, 2012. http://www.huffpost.com/entry/economic-consequences-of_b_1294430.

104 Howell, Kelly. "War and Economy." ScholarWorks@ GVSU. Accessed November 17, 2020. https://scholarworks.gvsu.edu/mcnair/vol15/iss1/4/.

been far-fetched, manipulated, or simply have not taken into account the economies of the countries involved, but rather the personal finances of very specific elements among its political and economic elite.

Cycles of peace and war

Wars can be caused by multiple factors, whereas we could say that peace conditions are maintained thanks to a delicate balance between many factors.

Factors such as oil have been at the center of multiple wars. To get an idea, there are estimates that between 25 and 50 percent of the wars between 1973 and 2012 were linked to oil geopolitics. These wars led to an increase in the price of oil. Such an increase has often been followed by periods of financial instability. However, in the same context, the rise in price generates large petrodollar profits, which are often invested in the arms race. The arms race favors conflicts that damage the infrastructure for oil production, pushing prices even higher.

Not all conflicts lead to an unstoppable spiral of rising oil prices, however. The price of oil is also a weapon that can be manipulated by oil-producing countries to break other oil adversaries, by pushing the price of oil down. This is a way of inflicting financial damage on geopolitical rivals with less capacity to resist a drop in revenues because of economic difficulties or excessive indebtedness.[105]

Multiple scholars have tried to find cyclical patterns in war, and the oil price cycle does not seem to

---

105 "War and the Oil Price Cycle." JIA SIPA, August 30, 2016. https://jia.sipa.columbia.edu/war-oil-price-cycle.

be the only associated factor. Cycles of war and peace are often related to the global economic cycle, as well as the political evolutionary process. The average time between large wars appears to be thirty-four years, with multiple small wars in between. The wars that have generated important transformations are spaced approximately fifty years apart, which coincides with the fifty-year cycle of major economic changes. Wars tend to occur during phases of economic recovery, since during economic depressions there is not enough liquidity to finance the cascade of expenses inherent to armed conflict.[106]

According to Harvard professor of political economy Benjamin Friedman, prolonged periods of economic hardship foster attitudes that feed social unrest. These attitudes can translate into terrorism, animosity towards minorities, and war.[107] In contrast, economic growth tends to reduce armed conflict.

Other, more daring scholars have proposed hypotheses such as the existence of a link between the solar cycle and war. While this may sound more like some pseudoscientific way of reading tea leaves, tarot cards or a horoscope, it might also be rash to discard them without first taking a closer look. There are times when we observe patterns we may think are due to

---

106 "Cyclical Warfare." Net Wars, August 27, 2007. https://netwar.wordpress.com/2007/08/26/cyclical-warfare/.

107 Davis, Lewis S., and Matthew Knauss. "The Moral Consequences of Economic Growth: An Empirical Investigation." *The Journal of Socio-Economics* 42 (2013): 43–50. https://doi.org/10.1016/j.socec.2012.11.007.

simple coincidence. However, rather than looking for a mystical or metaphysical correlation, it makes sense to consider that there may be variables involved. For example, the temperature of the planet can be associated with climate change. Climate change can affect agricultural production and water availability. Climate change can even affect the economy in many ways. These changes can spur new patterns of migration, which in turn can alter human demographic behavior and generate conflicts between groups. All of this suggests the need to observe such patterns carefully and make a well-reasoned analysis, should the statistics show a real correlation between the variables.

The race between powers

In the first half of the twentieth century, humanity witnessed two world wars, which some theorists describe as a single war with a ceasefire of almost twenty years in between. The confrontations left a toll of at least 17 million dead in the first war, and 65 million in the second.[108]

The reasons for engaging in armed conflict have varied across cultures and over time. It is said, for example, that the Crusades were motivated by fanaticism, prejudice, and a peculiar concept of honor. Some scholars claim that World War I occurred, basically, for four reasons (not very different from the causes that led to World War II): a tradition of militarism, close alliances between powers, imperialism, and nationalism.

---

108 "Segunda Guerra Mundial." Guerra Total. Accessed November 17, 2020. http://www.guerratotal.com/.

Militarism was a necessary result of imperialism, in order to maintain control over colonized territories. In turn, territorial imperialism was necessary to gain the advantage over other powers through the acquisition of raw materials and labor to maintain the vigorous growth of industrial development. Imperialism was also necessary to enlarge the free market zone that would support the growth of the economies of developed countries, at a time when strong global institutions had not been established to regulate or stimulate trade.

In the last years of World War II, the United States entered the conflict for fear that if its European allies were defeated, the US would have to deal with or even confront a unipolar Europe.

Since the two world wars, the closest we have been to a major armed conflict has been during the Cold War, which in reality was not as cold as many believe. We now know that the world was on the verge of nuclear war several times during this period, when the Soviet and Western blocs maintained a passive confrontation in a fierce and constant struggle for ideological, economic, and political expansion, mixed with a resurgence of colonialism. And while there was no direct confrontation between powers, there was a proliferation of armed conflicts in every corner of the world, fueled by the interests of both blocs. The Cold War came to an end for multiple reasons, among which historians highlight the Soviet war in Afghanistan, political changes in Eastern Europe, and economic decline in the Soviet Union, which did not allow it to maintain the arms race against the United States. All of these events contributed to the collapse of the Soviet Union, with a tacit acceptance of the failure of the communist system.

Looking back, the Cold War kept the world on the brink of an armed disaster for almost 40 years without a major conflict between the main powers. Strange, isn't it? How can such a tense situation be sustained for so long? The answer is simple: the ones doing the calculations on both sides realized that there was no better alternative than to maintain the status quo. This is where the concept of MAD (Mutual Assured Destruction) comes in. MAD is the guarantee that in the event of a hugely destructive attack, there will be a counterattack at least as destructive. It is ironic that, viewed dispassionately, nuclear proliferation has been an important (if not the main) reason for the relative peace in the world, at least among the superpowers. From the first years of the Cold War, it was known that any open confrontation between the powers would revive the use of nuclear weapons, which, according to everyone's calculations, would be so catastrophic that it would not be worth it. It is better to support factions on a smaller scale, in less industrialized, non-nuclearized nations, as an indirect challenge to the interests of a rival power. This seems to be the reason why, since World War II, the wars have only been between small countries, or between large powers and disproportionately weaker countries.

The Cold War has also taught us that fights do not necessarily have to involve the exchange of direct blows between opponents. It can also be seen as a shoving match between puppeteers to see who gets to pull the strings.

Meanwhile, national priorities have been changing. While in World War I the priorities were expansionism, imperialism, and territorial struggles, today, military interests have aligned with economic interests, and the support of the powers lies with the interests of their transnationals.

Economic interests have become intertwined with political interests in a globalization in which countries are increasingly dependent on the international community. This means that increasingly, going to war can result in self-inflicted economic injury, or even the loss of the raw materials necessary for the growth of a nation's own industries.

However, the tradition of forming alliances for armed confrontations between blocks of industrialized countries, which gave us two world wars, is a model that could shape future open conflicts between the North Atlantic Treaty Organization (NATO) and a potential alliance of Asian countries.

Traditionally, US and Russian achievements are credited to their highly developed military presence, while China has developed as an emerging power mainly through its commercial activity. However, the US is entering the arena of cold battle with a China that increases its military might by leaps and bounds, in a growing tension that we do not know how or where will end.

While territorial imperialism has become less common, a new form of imperialism has appeared, a neo-imperialism dominated by the expansion of large corporations in a tailor-made global free market where the only right that prevails is that of enrichment, regardless of the cost. Militarism continues to be the backbone of the powers, but for the purpose of defending the interests of their transnationals in their corporate expansion process.

Although the statistics from the two world wars are chilling and the historical events supposedly drove key changes that have given way to our current global society, you could say that they were just another war. Their main distinction was that they involved almost all of the industrialized nations of the planet at the time. The countries involved brought to the conflict their full capacity for innovation and mass industrial production. Surely it will not be the last great war, although history will be defined by the powers, with their ability to negotiate and shape global society. Today, there are developing countries that could become disruptive to the global order and have the potential to insert themselves among the traditional powers of the last centuries. This process is normal and expected as the gap between countries narrows on the way to a more egalitarian global community.

A new style of war

Evaluating the possibility of a new world war involves examining not only the potential causes, but also the potential styles.

A study conducted at the Siberian Federal University found that students' concept of modern war was associated with nuclear war and cyber warfare. The weapons of modern warfare were identified as the media, conventional weapons, the internet, and nuclear weapons.[109]

---

109 Koptseva, Natalia P., and Kseniya V. Reznikova.

Currently, we are living in a new arms race, but this time it's a technological one, where certain groups try to gain the technological advantage while others strive to close the gap or exceed their rival's capabilities. Naturally, legal regulations are always running to catch up with the capabilities developed by technology, in order to properly regulate them.

Technological advances in artificial intelligence in recent years could lay the groundwork for relevant changes to the rules of the game, redefining the global power balance. Silent cyber warfare is already a reality, while innovative technologies are not only aligning themselves in the service of war, but also making the manufacture (even by hand) of more lethal weapons easier. The use of unmanned weapons can lead to greater atrocities by terrorists, since it lends an anonymous touch to the attack, making it increasingly difficult to identify the author.

It is true that certain inventions developed for military use have gone on to make great contributions to our quality of life, such as the global positioning system (GPS). It is also true that military development consumes more than 60 percent of the research and development budget of the United States.[110]

"Modern War as a Cultural Phenomenon. Causes of War. Results of the Associative Experiment with 'Modern War' Associate (Based on Research Carried Out in the Student Groups of Siberian Federal University)." *Journal of Siberian Federal University. Humanities & Social Sciences* 8, no. 8 (2015): 1591–1610. https://doi.org/10.17516/1997-1370-2015-8-8-1591-1610.

110 "Defense to Get Historically High Share of Research Budget." Roll Call. Accessed November 17, 2020. https://

On the other hand, it seems that a nuclear war would no longer have the limitations that were factored into the calculations during the Cold War. The powers are developing new nuclear weapons, in the revival of a dangerous race.[111]

As if all this were not enough, it now turns out that a small nuclear war could even "benefit" climate change, in terms of reversing global warming.[112]

In a book on revolutions, a chapter on conflicts between powers may seem somewhat out of place. The point is that it is very difficult to understand the majority of revolts and revolutions without placing them in the context of competition between powers. The superpowers, with some frequency, are the hands that weave the threads of social unrest, as a way of competing to increase their dominance outside their borders.

I would like to finish this chapter with some personal observations that give me cause to believe we are approaching a third world war.

---

www.rollcall.com/2017/08/03/defense-to-get-historically-high-share-of-research-budget/.

111 "The Nuclear Arms Race Is Back...and Ever More Dangerous Now." The Guardian. Guardian News and Media, August 17, 2019. http://www.theguardian.com/world/2019/aug/17/nuclear-arms-race-is-back-and-more-dangerous-than-before.

112 Choi, Charles Q. "Regional Nuclear War Could Trigger Global Cooling and Famine." National Geographic, March 8, 2019. https://www.nationalgeographic.com/news/2011/2/110223-nuclear-war-winter-global-warming-environment-science-climate-change/.

Evidence that we might be approaching a huge war:

1. Divergent interests among superpowers.
2. A global authority is lacking at a time when no one respects the United Nations, which has become bureaucratic, inefficient, and virtually inoperative in many respects.
3. We are still far from the ideal unipolar world we imagined after the Cold War.
4. Multiple first world powers are expected emerge in the next 100 years (e.g., China and India).
5. Unstable alliances (there are still indirect conflicts between powers in peripheral nations).
6. There is no clearly superior military power, at a time when military spending does not necessarily translate into military effectiveness.
7. Military spending exceeds health spending and education spending.
8. The arms race continues, including nuclear weapons.
9. The technological arms race (autonomous weaponry) represents a large investment of resources in weapons whose effectiveness is not easily proven without a real armed conflict.

Atomic mushroom cloud over the Japanese city
of Nagasaki. Photo attributed to Sergeant George
Caron, in 1945.

Chapter 11:
Power in the hands of the masses

"Be strong and courageous. Do not be afraid or terrified because of them, for the Lord your God goes with you; he will never leave you nor forsake you."

— Deuteronomy 31:6

Populists are always talking about the great majority and the masses; in the same way, socialism is always talking about the people. But, what are the masses? Whom do they consist of? Where is the limit that defines whether I am part of the masses or not? How was that limit set? Why is it there? And who made the decision to include or exclude me?

To be honest, I have yet to find out the benefits of the latest populist discourse or the advantages of communism.

However, it seems somewhat hypocritical to criticize economic aid to the poorest without criticizing the connections of the richest. While it is true that interpersonal relationship skills are a lucrative talent worthy of ascension within any power structure, it is also true that when social connections are the only quality with value, the principle of meritocracy—which we believe leads to the betterment of humanity—is affected. An example of using interpersonal connections to climb over more talented or more deserving subjects is what George Soros, one of the richest men on the planet, calls "intelligent nepotism."

In the chapter on reality surpassing fiction, I mentioned at least one example in which a well-connected individual was able to mutate within their network of contacts throughout successive administrations, in order to keep on doing business within the legal parameters but without regard for morality or any sense of decency. I would go so far as to say that the well-connected do not change, they simply reinvent themselves to continue with their same practices based on the exchange of favors, thereby guaranteeing that appointments, contracts and concessions are awarded to close friends and family. This is exactly what a former Panamanian president referred to when he spoke of "friends of the presidential chair" or "leeches."[113]

The rules of the game are established by the few, regardless of the current social or economic system. It is a fact that the success or failure of every society falls largely on its political, economic, social and intellectual elites. While those at the top of the pyramid like to point their finger at those at the bottom, the blame usually

---

113 "Martinelli: 'Pipo' Es Amigo De La Silla." Inicio. Crítica, June 25, 2015. https://www.critica.com.pa/nacion-al/martinelli-pipo-es-amigo-de-la-silla-396765.

lies with the former, for one simple reason: they have a greater capacity to generate and effect change, since they possess most of the financial resources, time, education, and contacts necessary to form alliances with other members of the elite.

Perhaps, dear reader, it is very hard for you to even imagine the approximately 1,000 kilos of one-dollar bills, or the approximately 10 kilos of 100-dollar bills, which make up $1 million in cash;[114] or perhaps you are part of the 1 percent of the world population who may be frustrated to have such a paltry number of zeros in the combined value of your assets. What I don't think is hard for you to imagine is that those who have more resources also have more opportunities to effect social change.

However, this section of the book is not exactly about wealth distribution. Rather, I want to dedicate it to true power, the power of education and of the capacity for reasoning that we all possess, although many of us keep it locked away, latent, unused, as if it could be lost or damaged.

Many times the forces that define the balance within the structure of social power blend together within the debate, taking the form of religious, ethnic, partisan, cultural, or political struggles, among others. In reality, what is sought is the control of social power or more equitable conditions between different groups. Now, if cosmologists say that the universe is 73 percent dark energy of an unknown nature, and 23 percent dark

114 "How Much Actually Weigh...1 Million US Dollar?" How much does a million euro weigh? Accessed November 17, 2020. https://1000000-euro.de/how-much-does-a-million-dollars-weigh/index.php.

matter also of an unknown nature, what is the probability of achieving a complete understanding and mastery of the nature of human behavior?

We think we know a lot as a species. However, just in my small field of expertise—the human eye—there are all kinds of examples of how limited our understanding of nature really is. Only a little more than 100 years ago the anatomist and Nobel in medicine, Santiago Ramon y Cajal, described the structure of the tissue of the human retina. It was cause for euphoria, since the foundations of the best-studied part of the brain were being understood. However, 100 years later we are not yet able to fully understand how the retina actually works, much less regenerate or transplant it. The challenge will remain for future generations.

The problem is that when we do not understand something but insist on believing that we do, we fill our void in information with all kinds of prejudices and beliefs typical of our filter bubble (of which we are often unaware). Once we have satisfactorily (for us) filled that void with biases and distortions of reality, we tend to make mistakes, mistakes that can be terrible for others, as well as for ourselves.

In fact, I would say that an uninformed and belligerent society is worse than an idiot with initiative. Unfortunately, this type of situation is not uncommon in our day, with the daily bombardment we receive of half-truths and half-lies from all possible forms of digital communication.

I've seen a good example of this in my own country, Panama. The unspoken assumption by the richest that those least favored by fortune are a subclass of humanity has led to public policies that condemn the lower classes to a downward spiral of poverty and hopelessness. As a result, the country occupies twelfth position on the list of the world's most unequal countries, according to the World Bank's 2015 GINI index. It comes as no surprise that the underprivileged are practically excluded from any decision making, on the grounds that they do not have enough education, an education of which they have been deprived in an exclusive system. As a result, you have learned hopelessness on the one hand, and on the other, latent resentment towards the most affluent. The same story is repeated in many parts of the world, and of course, seems to be a common denominator throughout Latin America.

I remember that on one occasion, a friend who was doing a political marketing study told me about the impact a statement by one of the participants in a focus group had on him: "My grandparents were poor, my parents are poor, I am poor, and my children will be poor."

Naturally, learned hopelessness leads the masses to make perverse decisions (as if the information gap were not enough). Decisions such as supporting a position of "he stole but at least he got things done," where the populist discourse of an authoritarian leader nourishes the popular sentiment of "he screwed us all, but I'm glad he screwed the rich who have their foot on my head." This sentiment is all the more palpable when the lower strata see a possible way out of their condition through political corruption, which enables them to ascend within the social structure as executing elements of patronage and populism.

Hopelessness can lead people to do things that are hard to understand. In fact, it is not surprising that another country with poor social mobility, Colombia, has had more than 170,000 hectares planted with coca plants. Such an activity can only be understood as the only escape route from a system that marginalizes an important sector of the population.

It is striking that Bill Gates, despite being one of the richest men on the planet, points out that the inequities in today's societies are the product of unequal opportunities. So what opportunities is he referring to? Is it to seize all of the wealth and distribute it equally? Probably not. When talking about opportunities for the development of the individual, we are more likely to be referring to social mobility.

Social mobility is understood as the probability of moving up or down economically, both throughout life and from one generation to the next. The problem is that moving up is particularly difficult in the poorest countries.[115]

Educational mobility is not synonymous with income mobility. While reducing inequities in education does seem to play a role in closing the gaps between rich and poor, a system of meritocracy must be firmly established in order for a society's citizens to develop. Although it is easy to blame cultural heterogeneity for barriers to social mobility, social exclusion and labor

---

115 "Fair Progress? Economic Mobility across Generations Around the World." World Bank. Accessed November 17, 2020. http://www.worldbank.org/en/topic/poverty/publication/fair-progress-economic-mobility-across-generations-around-the-world.

discrimination exert a larger effect (here, some of the elements explored in chapter six, "The leader," come to mind). At this point, we may very well ask whether the lack of social development truncates meritocracy, or is it the lack of meritocracy that truncates social development? Perhaps it is simply a vicious circle.

It is precisely such barriers—the product of discrimination—that create unequal opportunities within society. What we often ignore is that the inequities produced by these barriers slowly undermine social trust.

In 2018, an article in the prestigious journal *Scientific American* highlighted that social trust is an important asset in every society, which once lost is very difficult to recover. In countries with the greatest inequality, social trust in institutions is even lower, which only hinders the adoption of policies aimed at reducing inequities. It has been suggested that social inequities and corruption intensify distrust within society and thwart social mobility. Without trust, it is more difficult to make any kind of change, and without change, it is very difficult to improve the situation. To put it another way, it is more difficult for a discredited political class to ask for more taxes for greater social investment,[116] even when social investment benefits everyone in one way or another.

So, in an environment where no one trusts anyone, distrust also finds a nice little niche in the void of

---

116 Rothstein, Bo. "How the Trust Trap Perpetuates Inequality." Scientific American. Scientific American, November 1, 2018. https://www.scientificamerican.com/article/how-the-trust-trap-perpetuates-inequality/.

information within the minds of the populace, further complicating matters.

All of this suggests that corruption hinders social mobility, which is true. But the lack of social mobility also seems to perpetuate corruption. According to a report by the Association of Public Accountants, countries with less social mobility are more susceptible to corruption. The reason is simple: if members of a few elite families have the best opportunities to occupy the best public positions, social mobility is truncated and greater corruption is perceived within the system.[117]

If, on top of everything else, the social *crème de la crème* that already dominates the public sector also dominates the private sector, there will be even less social mobility, and public-private corruption networks will be woven more tightly. Such networks are common and widespread throughout the world. These give rise to what is known in popular culture as *"a government of the banks, by the banks and for the banks"* (without detracting from the importance of banking in the economic and social development of modern economies).

In the end, everything is interconnected, with one element leading to another, and different aspects of society interacting with each other.

I remember that at some point I had an exchange of opinions with some anti-corruption activist friends.

---

117 https://www.accaglobal.com, ACCA -. "The Link between Poor Social Mobility and Corruption." ACCA Global. Accessed November 17, 2020. https://www.accaglobal.com/in/en/member/member/accounting-business/2019/01/insights/social-mobility.html.

We were discussing the best way to fight corruption, and the option of supporting honest candidates with a good track record and adequate preparation was raised. That is, to fight corruption, citizens must be made to vote for decent people who have demonstrated good values, honesty and sound moral underpinnings. The idea didn't sound bad. If corrupt politicians are the problem, let's make people choose honest politicians. However, on that occasion, I opposed such an initiative for one simple reason: corruption is not restricted to the sphere of politics. Corruption is part of the social fabric, and its consolidation among politicians, rather than indicating a personal attitude bereft of morals, is a manifestation of a social phenomenon which usually requires further study to better understand it. Naturally, most of the candidates who won the elections at the time of this discussion were not precisely those with the highest moral character.

The simple fact is that the issue of corruption cannot be addressed without confronting the issue of social mobility. It is very difficult to deliver an anti-corruption message when power is monopolized by a handful of families who do not have the slightest idea of what it means to have basic needs go unmet, and whose understanding of society is somewhere along the lines of the most odious form of apartheid.

When any elite person is asked what they would think of someone from the lowest social class taking the reins of power, they immediately dismiss such a possibility in their response. Why? Because they lack critical thinking? Because they don't share the same interests? Or do they fear the consequences of the social resentment harbored by the group that has been kept on the margins? Perhaps the answer is all of the above. What we do not see is that the rise of the marginalized classes is precisely what has happened and is happening in many parts of the world. It will probably even happen in the global community. It's just a matter of time.

Unfortunately, and though regarded unfavorably by most people, access to popularly elected office is one of the few options available to certain layers of society to climb within the social fabric when there is inadequate social mobility. Of course, the political ascent of such individuals will be accompanied by all kinds of populist speeches, while their ultimate goal will be evidenced by their actions: to enrich themselves at any cost.

Because corruption is a complex problem with multiple social, cultural, and economic facets, there is no way to end it without the collective will to rethink the social contract. Keep in mind that a change in the social contract, in itself, can be understood as a revolution.

It is assumed that democratic systems are based on the freedom of the individual. However, freedom cannot be exercised without information, options from which to choose, and the power to choose per se.

The debate lies in what information an individual must have to make decisions, information that is supposed to be provided by your education. Education is a topic that is always in fashion, but on which there is never consensus. Naturally, industrialists will say that education should be geared towards generating the necessary labor to improve production and meet the needs of economic growth. Laborers help the economy grow, which is not bad. The middle class, on the other hand, will hold the position that education must equip their children with the necessary tools to challenge the control of the dominant elite.

But...what about critical thinking? Isn't that education? And isn't that exactly what has produced the greatest advances in history? Unquestionably, to confront corruption requires cultural changes that must be addressed from grade school, including the development of attitudes towards possible acts of corruption and an understanding of the damage that corruption causes to society. However, individual freedom is only achieved through the ability to doubt, question, reason, think objectively and seek the truth.

The ability to question is what led to the understanding that there is no such thing as spontaneous generation, after centuries of arguing that certain living beings could be generated as a product of non-living, unrelated material. To this very day, the inability to question and reason has caused a good chunk of humanity to remain steeped in a wide range of popular beliefs and folklore.

I remember one of my professors in medical school telling us: "A donkey knows more by asking, than a wise man by answering." However, it seems that things are changing. Today, there is so much free access to information that it is easier for us to obtain and share (including through social networks) information, than to question the information provided to us.

The ability to question what we read is valuable for understanding situations at all levels. Even when reading biblical passages, like any other holy book, interpretations vary widely among people. That is, although there is the same faith, the same formation, two individuals can hold a different understanding of certain concepts that they believe to be unquestionable. This variability occurs because the transmitted knowledge must also be processed by the human neurophysiological filter (which varies between individuals), as well as interact with previous knowledge, personal experiences, etc. Some will adopt a figurative understanding, while others (usually those with a narrower range of experiences) lean towards a literal interpretation. In the end, it is part of the freedom of thought with which each human being is endowed.

In other words, apart from the technical knowledge and skills that an individual can develop, transformative thinking on social issues will come from enlightenment and from the ability to develop critical thinking. And it is this critical thinking that will hopefully enable people to communicate in the development of creativity and the analysis needed to solve problems. But this can only happen if we keep an open mind to question the truth of our own thoughts and beliefs.

The greatest weapon against populism, corruption, plutocracies, monopolies, oligarchies, etc., is a new enlightenment that reaches the majority of citizens. More than in belligerence and social activism, power lies in education and critical thinking.

Critical thinking prevents the members of a society from falling prey to manipulation, while at the same time encouraging greater social participation. There are even psychological studies that correlate citizen participation with empowerment. Psychological empowerment is described as a connection between the sense of personal competence and the desire and intention to take action in the public domain, and is directly associated with taking on positions of leadership.[118]

To conclude this chapter, I want to emphasize that if we look back, all the examples of revolutions mentioned in chapter three have been accompanied by a profound change in the concepts previously understood by society. The Renaissance certainly involved an intense flow of information, which led to drastic changes in the views of the era. The Enlightenment was perhaps not so much a movement of information as a new structuring in the way of thinking, which served to quickly spread the ideas of freedom. In the same way, the successive industrial revolutions have responded to the generation of new knowledge in the different fields of engineering, supported by the advances of science. Even the advances that amaze us so much today and are revolutionizing our daily lives are the product of scientific and technological breakthroughs that were years in the making.

Revolutions with political nuances have also responded to transformations in thought. The Russian Revolution was accompanied by a new ideology that had been taking shape over decades. The French Revolution, likewise, sprang from a platform of thought on which the power of the kings was challenged. The American Revolution also responded to changes in mentality and ideas of freedom fostered by the Enlightenment.

---

118 Camerini, Luca, and Peter Johannes Schulz. "Effects of Functional Interactivity on Patients' Knowledge, Empowerment, and Health Outcomes: An Experimental Model-Driven Evaluation of a Web-Based Intervention." *Journal of Medical Internet Research* 14, no. 4 (2012). https://doi.org/10.2196/jmir.1953.

The question of whether or not there is violence, or whether the interests of the rich or the poor are being promoted, is not really relevant. It is not relevant whether lobbying is being conducted through the media, or weapons or money are being handed out. The only thing truly capable of challenging a dominant power is an open mind and a change in the way of thinking. It seems that human thought is able to travel further than bullets, and explode more sharply than Molotov cocktails.

I want to close this chapter with the following question: If freedom implies options from which to choose, the ability to make choices, and information to assist in making those choices, can we really say that we in our western societies are free? Do we really have options? Do we really have the ability to make decisions about our environment? Or do we simply have the necessary and adequately structured information, but no way to apply it?

Chapter 12:
Reflections

"Of all the frictional resistances, the one that most retards human movement is ignorance."

— *Nikola Tesla*

In the introduction, I apologized if any position in this book makes you uncomfortable. If your views are different, I respect that, and I invite you to reflect on the following: differences of thought and respect for different ways of thinking or understanding the world are what enable a society to approach its problems with maturity.

As an activist medical student, I remember attending a workshop of the International Federation of Medical Students Associations (IFMSA) hosted in conjunction with the United Nations, where we were told that differing viewpoints should be met not with tolerance, but respect: respect that accepts the other point of view without making a judgment on who is right or wrong. Divergences of opinion are the product of complex situations, experiences, and even neurological aspects that I explain best in my previous book, *From Primates to Politicians*.

It is precisely that sense of respect for others that makes the continued existence—seventy-five years after WWII—of neo-Nazi groups and debates around nationalist, racist, or anti-immigration policies, seem like a hallucination.

Our human limitations

If we are going to place a value on our existence, I have thought that the most valuable thing we have in life is time. Not only to share with our loved ones or to develop professionally, financially, or socially; time is valuable because it limits us in what we can achieve throughout our lives.

Time limits practically everything we do. For example, if we wanted to eradicate poverty, we could work hard on it, but most likely we will die without seeing it. Once poverty is eradicated, new challenges will appear, which will again require time that we do not have in our short lives to see them to fruition.

However, to understand the universe, or simply the world, or even less...to be able to question and understand our immediate surroundings, the main limitation is not time but the capacity of our own brain.

Astrophysicist Carl Sagan said that the universe and the laws that govern it exceed the processing capacity of the human brain. I am acutely aware of this in my own profession. What little I know I use every day to try to help other human beings preserve their vision, with all the satisfaction that comes from seeing the smile of someone who could not see and is once again able to recognize the faces of loved ones, reread their favorite books, etc. But I know that I will never understand the full range of biological, physical and chemical phenomena that occur within an eye, and I will certainly never have the processing capacity to understand them all at once. In fact, humanity as a whole will probably never have the storage capacity to understand all the biological, physical and chemical processes that occur within the eye of one of my patients.

Critical thinking

We perceive our surroundings in ways that sometimes contradict reality. Part of this distorted view of reality can be transmitted to us by the perception of those who share our surroundings, acting like a magnet that brings the different members of a group closer together, where they mutually reinforce the distorted perception (as in the case of groupthink). Together, we make wrong decisions which we cling to and defend in order to feel good (the anchoring process). We can see this in business groups, unions and the like.

Science has shown that the introduction of critical thinking into politics, using the scientific method, leads to more effective and efficient decisions and a greater well-being for all.

The expression "critical thinking" has been mentioned repeatedly throughout this book. Before ending, a definition of this concept is in order. Critical thinking refers to the structuring of information so that logical connections are established between ideas. This allows us to solve complex problems systematically, and to subject our beliefs and values to a critical assessment. Critical thinking is what allows us to understand that the topics of debate are rarely simple, but a network of multiple interconnected factors. It is what allows us to understand that there is no radical and rapid solution to migration, to gender issues, to crime, to wars, to the economic model, etc. Without a doubt, critical thinking is necessary for the development of any liberal democracy. If citizens do not develop the ability to think critically about social problems, they will have no idea of what a good government is, and will be incapable of selecting good rulers or contrasting the actions that benefit society against their own prejudices.

Science: instrument and victim of change

Knowledge, together with different viewpoints, options from which to choose, and the possibility of choosing, acting and expressing oneself without being harassed or persecuted, is what is called freedom. However, commodification is generating distortions in the generation of knowledge. Evidence of this distortion can be seen in what is currently happening with the basic sciences, which appear to be abandoning the quest for a better understanding of who we are, to focus most of their resources on technological development at the exclusive service of free enterprise. Not that it is wrong to innovate and develop free enterprise; the problem is when the generation of knowledge is placed at the mercy of money.

We see the benefits of science in every detail of our lives. Today, almost all of us carry a cell phone. Space exploration has given us formulas for feeding babies, hand-held vacuum cleaners for our cars, cochlear implants for the deaf, infrared thermometers, digital cameras, and anti-scratch plastic lenses. Sadly, the space program today has been contaminated to the point where economic and military interests have prevailed, setting aside all the impact it initially achieved. As a result, space exploration seems to have been relegated to a chapter in the history books, replaced by the development of artificial intelligence and interconnection, or other more profitable businesses. The situation has been exacerbated by the entry of other countries into the space race. Instead of trying to solve the problems we are creating on the planet, or looking for ways to survive the potential threats we might face, space is now regarded as a source of minerals, a business, or worse, a scenario to export our stupidities, such as war between nations.

Selfishness and impunity

Our environment is constantly changing, with every turn opening the door for a new revolution. The way each society deals with change depends entirely on the collective perception of reality and the dynamics of the interactions among its members. It depends on the ability to transfer the ideals of enlightenment and to organize in order to challenge the status quo. Both aspects—the spread of enlightenment and the structuring of civil society—are the target of political control, and constantly undermined in modern western societies, where they drown in the selfish interests of the individual members.

Selfish interests can lead each of us to jail or to the choicest places in society, in a way that not even the best fiction writers could come up with. It is difficult to appeal to the collective feeling of belonging to society or to invoke solidarity while we are flooded with petty success stories and great achievements that reward selfish individuality. It seems that the main obstacle to social change in any society is the ability of the elite to adjust the size of the rod with which their actions are measured, while applying one of disproportionate dimension to the rest of society. Although judicial precepts establish equality under the law, it is well known that the law is interpreted according to the resources and influence of the defendant. This is repeated in all kinds of political systems: authoritarian, democratic, capitalist, socialist, etc. The only thing that varies is how much the rod can be adjusted.

For this reason, it can be said that impunity is and will continue to be the main obstacle in any fight against organized crime. Criminal organizations commit illegal acts precisely because they are profitable. Such profitability facilitates their insertion into the circles of power, providing access to the webs already spun between politicians and corrupt businessmen, where the party has already started and everyone knows how to dance to the same rhythm.

The race for control

Coincidentally, the group that is measured with the adjustable rod is also the first to attack those who challenge the existing order, through intimidation or attempts to control the spread of sentiment among the masses, activities for which they already possess a high level of "expertise."

It is precisely around sentiment that interests will diverge. Emotions cause the masses to become enraged, and those who are best able to manage a group's emotions will usually occupy the positions of leadership in the group. It is this ability to manage the emotions of the group that will turn an ordinary person into an enemy of the State or public order. The irony is that is easier for such an individual to become part of the "establishment" than to unite a group to achieve social transformation.

The race for the control of collective emotions leads to a competition to shape our mental wiring or to create a collective illusion that best suits the interests of the opposing parties. In the end, the masses will only place their belief in the most widely publicized or most convincing illusion, which does not necessarily respond to reality.

Competition for the control of collective illusion is accompanied by infiltration in every detail of our lives, from politics, media, and our social networks, to the apps on our electronic devices. They are all pieces in what has become a game to extract benefits from each one of us without our conscious consent.

Such is the effect of the influence exerted over our mental wiring and behavior, that we have adopted consumption patterns that could endanger our very existence without a revolution to prevent it. With each passing day we have more evidence, but less awareness, of our fragility as living beings on planet Earth, a fragility that can only be grasped through an appreciation of the extraordinary coincidence of multiple factors that allows us to be here, writing, or reading this book.

And how do we honor this fragility? By racing to achieve the power to destroy, to consolidate economic and social control. It is a race that goes hand in hand with the technological developments we so love to boast about, every time some new "autonomous" object appears with the capability of causing mass destruction among "brothers." Some see this as a game, an opportunity to try out their new "toys" and secure a victory, to gratify their own ego, or fill their own pockets.

Obviously, ordinary people may not be aware of how their environment is being manipulated, but they are surely aware that their quality of life is not everything they hoped it would be. Truncated desires can lead social groups to "do something," something that does not necessarily have to be good or positive for everyone in society. Frustration can lead to feelings of resentment, social polarization, and even a thirst for revenge, which can be exploited by...let's guess... politicians from different ideological currents? Radical activists? Different economic forces? Or powers playing their geo-political game?

Challenging the system

The only true revolutions are those achieved through education and subsequent empowerment. Violent revolutions, without education or structuring of thought, only produce a change of tyrant. Many revolutions, in the end, have been nothing more than vague illusions, reminiscent of the fable in which a carrot is dangled in front of the donkey to get it to pull the cart. In the political game, the dangling carrot takes different forms: populist discourse, the radical oratory of a "strongman," a promise of better days, or simply a dream of better times to come.

There is a term used in political and military science: strategic stability. This term refers to the probability of effectively inducing some change to the status quo. A good analogy for understanding strategic stability is to observe the behavior of a marble in a soup ladle. No matter how we move the marble inside the ladle, it will return to the same spot. In the same way, there are social conditions that give strategic stability to the current social structure. Corruption, ignorance, and social immobility are good examples of conditions that guarantee strategic stability in a Western society.

Systems can change: societies, economies, social development indicators, and even political and economic elites. The only thing that does not change is human nature, which moves within all of the above.

I hope this book does not leave you disappointed by the absence of incendiary speech or invitation to open violence. I am convinced that the only truly revolutionary act these days is to embrace and acquire the knowledge that, together with the ability to reason, leads us to free thinking.

The waves of the sea roll endlessly onto the beach. All carry with them sand and water, but no two are the same. Likewise, there are no two identical moments in history, or in each of our lives. Each moment as unique. We have only to wait for the next moment when freshly awakened minds emerge that are able to share the light with their peers, until a new social contract is achieved, in the next great...

REVOLUTION!

Acknowledgements

The publication of this book would not have been possible without the patience and support of my wife, Maria Teresa.

I am very grateful to my mother, Omayra, not only for her contributions to me as a human being and as a professional, but also for taking the time to read the draft and question the concepts. The entire concept review process led to a more interesting book.

To Ian Graham Leask, Gary Lindberg and the team at Calumet Editions, who, by trusting me as a writer, have allowed me to reach English-speaking readers who will surely enjoy analyzing problems and challenges that transcend time, language and borders.

To Rebecca Wentzel, who employed her extensive experience in translation of scientific material and great professionalism to translate this book into clear and fluent English. I have no way of thanking her for her patience and dedication in providing English speakers with the best possible rendering of the original.

I cannot end without thanking my fellow graduates of the International Federation of Medical Students (IFMSA), who were an important source of inspiration that led me become a doctor and political scientist. The only way to work to build a better world is by thinking globally and acting locally.

My gratitude to my colleagues in the Science Movement in Panama; every day I learn more from them about the value of science and education in the social transformation of my country.

I also want to thank my colleagues from the Kiwanis Club of Panama and the Independent Movement for Panama who have shown me that courage is a necessary civic value to defend freedom.

Last but not least, I want to thank you for reading this book. Without your interest and support, my efforts in writing this work would have been irrelevant.

About the Author

Juan Manuel Muñoz, born in Panama City, is a physician, political scientist, futurist, business administrator, musician, and social activist in the areas of human rights, pacifism, and a movement toward a sustainable environment. He began his participation as social activist during his medical studies at the University of Panama, which led him to sit on the executive board of the International Federation of Medical Students Associations (IFMSA). The current political uncertainty, along with fast-paced political changes, led Muñoz to publish multiple opinion articles in local newspapers, and finally to publish his first book, *From Primates to Politicians*.